calming your anxious child

A Biblical Game Plan for Parenting Through Big Emotions

calming your anxious child

A Biblical Game Plan for Parenting Through Big Emotions

micah maddox

Moody Publishers
CHICAGO

Published in association with the literary agency of Tracie Miles Literary.

Edited by Avrie Roberts
Cover design: Brittany Schrock
Interior design: Tammy Adelhardt
Cover graphic of watercolor circle copyright © 2026 by magnia/Adobe Stock (59065209). All rights reserved.
Interior graphic of armor of God copyright © 2026 by springartt/Adobe Stock (97047911). All rights reserved.
Interior graphic of emoticons copyright © 2026 by Pattern_Repeat/Adobe Stock (579365722). All rights reserved.

ISBN: 978-0-8024-3987-1

Originally delivered by fleets of horse-drawn wagons, the affordable paperbacks from D. L. Moody's publishing house resourced the church and served everyday people. Now, after more than 125 years of publishing and ministry, Moody Publishers' mission remains the same—even if our delivery systems have changed a bit. For more information on other books (and resources) created from a biblical perspective, go to www.moodypublishers.com or write to:

Moody Publishers
820 N. LaSalle Boulevard
Chicago, IL 60610

1 3 5 7 9 10 8 6 4 2

Printed in the United States of America

In honor of
Our Ray of Sunshine
Because I love ya.
God answers impossible prayers!

Contents

introduction

Healing is a journey and hope is possible. Those are the reasons I wrote this book. I believe that God can help you and your child start the path toward both today.

Hi, my name is Micah, and I am the mom of five children. Two of our children were adopted through foster care. In our home we have several diagnoses represented:

- Generalized anxiety disorder
- Autism spectrum disorder
- Developmental delays
- Reactive attachment disorder
- Post-traumatic stress disorder
- Neonatal abstinence syndrome
- Attention-deficit/hyperactivity disorder

Just to name a few. I know what it is like to struggle to help a child through an episode of overwhelm, a complete meltdown, a panic attack, a fit of rage, social fear, lack of sleep, and many other behaviors and struggles that children with anxiety face. I know what it's like to leave an event early or not go at all due to my child's battle with anxiety. I've protected a child from themselves as they attempt to deal with the feelings overtaking every part of their being. I've sought out professional help, administered medications and counted the pills, and practiced all the breathing techniques and changed diets. I know what it's like to fight every day to see a little ray of light and hope.

Speaking of a ray of light, our youngest son's name is Ray. He is high-functioning on the autism spectrum and has multiple other complicated mental health diagnoses. One of them is generalized anxiety disorder. He is fully aware that I have included him in this book. He even contributed a little "Ray of Sunshine" in each chapter for you and your child to enjoy together.

As a testimony of hope, I can share that Ray is learning to manage his anxiety. This is something in certain seasons we thought might never be possible. So for you, dear parent who feels like hope is out of reach, I am lending you my hand to walk along with you through these pages. My prayer is that you will find some help and hope that will reach right inside your heart and give it a little hug. Maybe you just need to hear that you and your child are going to be okay. Because I really believe you can be.

In *Calming Your Anxious Child*, we are going to slowly and simply walk through what it looks like to pray over and with your child in the moments of calm to help combat the moments of chaos through connection with God. This is a Bible-based, parent-to-parent book to encourage your heart on the days when you do not know what to do for your anxious child. I hope it feels like a "sideline" conversation—like with a coach you trust pulling you out of the game for a moment to give you the pep talk you need before sending you back in to secure the game-winning victory. This book was carefully and tenderly written for you, the parent who knows your child's struggle is anxiety or thinks it could be.

A Word About Doctors, Therapy, and Medication

Yes, professional help might be necessary. Make the appointment. Get the evaluation. Talk through the results. Consult a professional. Counseling, therapy, or medication might be a game changer. But there is something else on top of all that I want to offer you today: lasting hope for you and your family.

From one parent who gets it to another, all the best parenting in the world won't change a child's heart and mind toward true calm. Only God can do that. Sit back, take a deep breath, and let's stop striving so much. I see you doing your best. And when you don't know what to do, remind yourself God is the One who brings about lasting change.

Tools for Tired Parents

I've also included multiple quick and easy resources for you at the end of this book with more on my website, MicahMaddox.com. You'll find instructional videos, prayer calendars for on-the-spot daily prayers, and a few fun activities for you and your child to enjoy together.

part one

game plan for calming the body

chapter one

seeking calm

You are not failing. You love your child more than life itself and you simply want everything to be okay. If you are exhausted, burned out, and feel like no one understands, I see you. More than that, God sees you. He knows the late-night frustrations, the early morning battles, the middle-of-the-night wake-ups, and the impossible moments when you don't know what to do.

In these pages we will wrestle with the reality of loving a child so much you would do just about anything to help them through their anxious episodes. We will discover real-life solutions to help you move from unsettled, chaotic, and feeling like you can't do anything to help your child, to parenting with hope, confidence, and relief for both of you. While I will give you lots of ideas, the main thing that truly makes all the difference is the power of God over the anxieties present in your child's world.

The practice of speaking Bible truth over my children has been transformative for them and for me. It is simple, and the payout is miraculous because that is the kind of God we serve, a miracle-working one. It is not about the method or a special voice or stance, it is about the power of our amazing God and the way He answers prayers—*your* prayers. If you are desperate for help, hold on. Hope is on the way! After all, "Getting help isn't a sign of weakness—it's a sign of wisdom."[1]

Brace Yourself

When my child experiences anxiety, I can often see it a mile away. The way they walk, run, sit, or breathe tells me before they can. When anxiety rears its head, it comes out in sporadic body movements and a faster motor than typical excitement. You've seen this in your own child. Their little heart starts pumping harder. Hands start tapping, feet are swinging. Running into walls or tripping is common. Perhaps your child isn't quite as robust physically when it comes to big feelings, but you can see anxiety paralyzing or rising frantically in its own unique way.

You brace yourself for tears, an outburst, or for the complete shutdown. But rather than simply bracing yourself and letting anxiety be in the driver's seat, I want to empower you to pump the brakes and try something that really works. We will begin with our foundation of God's Word and work our way to communicating with God through prayer. This will be our model for every parenting tip in this book. Start with the Bible. Follow through by talking to God about it. With this simplified parenting style, you will be equipped and ready to wage war on your child's toughest anxiety battles. But even if you mess up or get off track, with the power of the Holy Spirit, you can get right back on track and try again.

When I asked my son Ray what the most important thing was that he had learned to help him manage his big feelings, he immediately said, "Stop. Breathe. Think."

These three words haven't always come easily for him, but they do now (most of the time), and they have helped him change chaos to calm, irrational fears to courage, and panic to peace beyond understanding. I don't exaggerate when I say God has transformed Ray's heart and mind in a miraculous way. It reminds me of that famous verse from Psalm 46.

> "Be still, and know that I am God.
> I will be exalted among the nations,
> I will be exalted in the earth!"
>
> (PSALM 46:10 ESV)

Be still. It is so much easier said than done. Can you count how many times you've tried to tell your child to sit still, calm down, or stop fidgeting or moving so much? I am learning that the movement of our bodies and our children's bodies tells us a lot about the feelings and emotions going on inside. For these uncertain moments when all you want to do is scream "BE STILL," we are going to replace this moment with these three words: **Stop. Breathe. Think.**

Go ahead and stop for a moment, take a few deep slow breaths, and open your heart to what God's Word has to say. Breathe in. Breathe out. Repeat as many times as you need. God designed our bodies to respond to breathing in remarkable ways! Scientific research confirms that breathing holds the power to help with:

- Calming the nervous system
- Positively affecting brain waves
- Aiding in pain response
- Assisting in sleep problems

- Helping the body to rest and digest
- Reducing stress responses[2]

When God created our breath, it was a gift. In Genesis 2:7, God "breathed into his nostrils the breath of life, and man became a living being." Breath is life-giving!

> While the external sources of fear may or may not rest, in God's presence we always can.

When we face external or internal stressors, our heart rate and breathing rates increase, our muscles tense, and we sweat more.[3] This is a real change that happens in the brain and body, and we should not ignore it in ourselves or our children. We cannot only address stress by expecting a child to snap out of it, nor can we simply slap a Band-Aid Bible verse on anxiety. We can best help our child by understanding the physiological impact of what they are experiencing as well as the power of God over it.

The idea we find in Psalm 46 is that God is the ruler over all, even over the problems and distresses within this world. As the psalmist gets to verse 10, he declares to all creation to quiet down and rest knowing God is Creator and King over all. It is not so much a command to the psalmist to be still, but a declaration to the *trouble that surrounds* the psalmist to be still.

We find this same idea in the story of the disciples on the sea when a great storm arose and Jesus tells the storm, "Peace! Be still!" (Mark 4:39 ESV). Jesus displays His miracle-working power by calming the external sources of fear and unrest—the wind and the waves. Only then does He address the human response of fear and lack of faith. When we realize and acknowledge God is able to calm the external anxiety driving sources of fear, we will be ready to take every fear to Him. While the external sources may or may not rest, in God's presence we always can.

The great hope these biblical examples offer us is that God did not command the disciples to hush and sit down, or inspire the psalmist to speak to the anxiety filling the human heart. Rather, in both cases we find God calming the surrounding stressors and offering a place of rest for the people in the narrative. Maybe you need rest right now too. This is your permission to take care of yourself and be still. Take a moment to remember God is in control of everything even when parenting feels impossible.

By acknowledging that God is in control of everything, even the wind and waves that feel like they are crashing all around them, we give our children a great gift. God is capable of calming every storm, whether the storm is seen like the lightning and rain, or unseen like thunder and wind, or the pounding of their own beating heart.

Let's take this Bible truth and apply it practically.

Stop, breathe, and think for yourself right now. How can you expect your child to stop, breathe, and think if you aren't thinking clearly or breathing slowly yourself? As one expert noted, "You cannot be upset if your breathing is slow, deep, quiet, and regular."[4] So go ahead and practice a few slow, deep, quiet breaths right now. Relax your shoulders. Let go of the tension in your jaw. Breathe in through your nose and out through your mouth until you feel a sense of calm.

Now, with your body, mind, and soul calm, you are ready to talk to your child. Do not jump into a chaotic moment and try to implement any idea in this book. If your soul is not in a calm place, you cannot lead your child toward calmness. Choose a quiet moment when all is well with both you and your child.

If your soul is not in a calm place, you cannot lead your child toward calmness.

Introduce the idea of *stop, breathe, and think* to your child as a tool you both are going to use when either of you feel overwhelmed, afraid, angry, or anxious. The more you prepare ahead of time, the better results and success you will have in the heat of the moment. I have provided guided questions and conversation you can have depending on your child's ability and understanding. Take it slow and only do as much as you and your child can do while keeping the experience positive.

1. Stop.

Ask the question: "What does it mean to stop?"

Example of an answer you can talk about: "Stopping means we pause like in a game or a movie. We stop what we are doing. We make our bodies still, and we don't say any more words. Let's practice right now."

Make it fun! Start your child's favorite show or game, pause it and show them how to freeze physically and literally stop what they are doing right away; play freeze tag or become a statue in the middle of doing a chore or activity.

Follow through: "This is what it means to stop. Let's practice."

2. Breathe.

Ask the question: "Who gives us breath?"

Example of an answer you can talk about: "God gives us every breath we breathe, so it is a gift. Our life literally relies on the breaths we take. One way we can honor God and thank Him for what He has given us is to take slow, deep, quiet breaths when we feel overwhelmed, angry, sad, or afraid. Let's practice right now. I'll go first."

Now have your child practice slow, deep, quiet breaths. For us, ten breaths seems to be our magic number. It gets us past the panic, fear, or intense anger. Your child might need more or less. You might find this helps you too! Sometimes if my child is extremely dysregulated, three breaths helps us get through the initial chaotic moment. Then we move slowly toward trying a few more breaths together. Give yourself a chance to figure out how it works best for you and your child.

Follow through: "Let's practice *stop*, *breathe* together." Repeat a few times before moving on.

3. Think.

Ask the question: "Who created your brain?"

Example of an answer you can talk about: "God made you so smart! The Bible says God created you wonderfully (Psalm 139:14). You have a good brain that can think about all kinds of amazing things. One thing that God wants us to think about is Him. When we let our brains think about how good and amazing God is, we don't worry so much. When we stop, breathe, and think, we can remember God can help us calm down. So next time you feel big feelings that make your heart beat harder, or your head or tummy hurt, I am going to say three words to help you think about God: Stop. Breathe. Think. Let's say them together right now. Stop. Breathe. Think."

Repeat and practice as many times as necessary to get this game plan ready to implement.

Follow through: This is something you can practice every day until it becomes something that your child begins to do on their own. Do not use one of the words alone unless the child is already too upset in an emotional spiral. Use all three words together every time—*stop, breathe, think*. Repeat these words calmly and slowly until things de-escalate. Attempt eye contact and say it again. Do not move on until calmness is setting in.

truth-telling time

Now it is time to apply the Bible truth by saying it out loud. This might mean you say a Bible verse and prayer, or it could simply be a Bible principle condensed into a few words. As you do this step, focus on *being with* your child rather than *responding to* your child.

The "I am with you" attitude is going to do wonders to get your child to stay regulated and in sync with you rather than fight against you.

It could look something like this: "I am with you and God's Word says, 'Be still and know that I am God.' God is here. Stop, breathe, think. Let's practice breathing together so we can think clearly about God."

At this moment, I would typically pray out loud over my child for the specific situation. It might look something like, "Dear God, please help [insert child's name] to be able to stop, breathe, and think when they feel overwhelmed by [insert fear or struggle]. Remind them You are stronger than [insert fear or struggle]. In Jesus' name, amen."

Repeat or continue praying until the child begins to relax.

☆ all-star tip

Use hand motions for this exercise. Start by holding one hand up in front of your shoulder, palm facing out, and say, "Stop." Next, place your hand on your chest, saying, "Breathe." Finally, pointing with one finger to your temple, say, "Think." Use this hand motion every time you use this game plan and your three words. Teach your child to do the same and practice together.

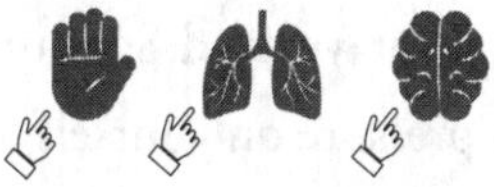

Prayer is our biggest weapon in our arsenal of parenting. You can read all the books (even this one), go to all the conferences, and do all the therapies, but without God's power you and your child will still be lacking the true help needed to overcome the difficult days. Through prayer, God continues to help us overcome and conquer many of the things that used to be a daily struggle.

Ray loves to write his prayers and is excited to share one with you in every chapter. Feel free to have your child read or write out Ray's prayers on a piece of paper. (If you do, be sure to send us a copy so Ray can see. You will make his day!) Ray's love of words and prayer is something we celebrate as part of his continual healing journey.

a ray of sunshine

Dear God, thank You for all of my blessings. I know that You are more powerful than anyone on earth. Please help me to stop in rough times and take a deep breath. Help me to stop and think when I am getting upset and about to react to my feelings. Help me to know that You are God and that You can help me even when it seems impossible. In Jesus' name, amen.

parent heart check

After you have tried to implement a truth-telling game plan, evaluate what went well and where things can improve or shift to be more successful. The power of prayer and Scripture are your key moves, so don't put too much pressure on yourself to produce results. Your main objective through these plans and practices is to focus on your relationship with God and the power He offers you to stay calm, focused, and under control. Instead of thinking, *God, fix my child*, think, *God, help me think clearly and stay calm.*

Questions to ask yourself:

- Did I stay calm?
- Did I lift my voice?
- Did my heartbeat escalate?

The goal of self-evaluation is not to beat yourself up, but rather to find areas where you can shift your methods to work for you rather than against you. Work on telling yourself the truth before, during, and after difficult moments so you are ready and prepared when things get tense. Let's move from self-evaluation to application. As you read through each of the following prompts, don't go too fast. This is where transformation can happen for you. Stop, breathe, and think deeply about the child that you love so much.

- Think about one character trait you love about your child.
- Think about one area your child is really struggling right now.
- Decide on a time you will talk to your child about "Stop. Breathe. Think."
- What time of day will work best for you and your child to practice this game plan?

- Take time to write in a journal or say out loud a prayer of gratitude to God for being in control of all, even your child's big feelings.

game plan highlights

- While the external stressors may or may not rest, in God's presence we always can.
- If your soul is not in a calm place, you cannot lead your child toward calmness.
- Instead of thinking, *God, fix my child*, think, *God, help me think clearly and stay calm.*

chapter two

magnetic words

I sat in another therapy session with my young child hoping for a tangible piece of advice to get us moving from chaos to calm. We were desperate for help . . . relief . . . answers. I was willing to do just about anything to help our son learn to cope with all the big feelings he had swirling within. We had tried everything we knew to do.

We walked away with a few words to say in moments of chaos, anxiety, or desperation. These words are widely used and known by many in the mental health field and there is a good reason why. Here they are:

"I see you."

"I hear you."

"I'm with you."

I began practicing saying these words. Over and over, I repeated them to my son when he was wrestling with big feelings.

I see you. I hear you. I'm with you.

I see you. I hear you. I'm with you.

While these aren't magic words, they are magnetic words. They help a child and parent move from divided and dysregulated to direct communication. Side by side, parent and child can begin to sync up together.

Magnetic words help you get down on your child's level. Eye to eye. Body facing body. Connection is the point. Or as one expert put it,

> In a phenomenon psychologists call *matching*, a mother and child synchronize their behavior, continually mimicking and mirroring each other's vocalizations, eye contact, body movement, posture, sleep cycles, and more. Attentive caretaking and matching helps cement the familial bond and build secure attachment, teaching the child important lessons.[1]

You've probably heard the phrase *connection over correction*. This is where we find magnetic words really taking action. *I see you, I hear you, I'm with you* statements and actions help forge a new path forward. They focus more on connecting with the child before redirecting them toward appropriate responses.

Anxiety is not typically a misbehavior as much as it is a misunderstood expression of fear.

Many will try to correct a behavior based on an outward explosion or visible offense, but the three sentences offered here give parents a pathway to peaceful connection amidst correction. Anxiety is not typically a misbehavior as much as it is a misunderstood expression of fear. While correction and coping skills must be put into place and practiced, the real traction will take place in the seeing, hearing, and being with your child. This is not permissive parenting, it is *proactive parenting*. It is all about giving your child the tools they need to cope before coping is necessary.

Connecting is not only about being with the child and providing tools, but also about mirroring or matching the child's body movements, voice, tone, and words. It may feel silly when you start it, the kind of thing only weak parents do. But as a mom of five who seemed to hold parenting in the palm of my hand until the fourth child, I found myself trying it with great success.

Before you read my magnetic words in action in the example below, it is vital to remember this was not an attempt to correct poor behavior. The goal was to help give my child tools to cope and come out of a cycle of extreme anxiety. His pretend play took him to a safe place far away from reality. The type of play he was exhibiting was not a healthy display of childhood fun and imagination. There were unhealthy behaviors that needed attention and redirection.

You can identify your child's own unhealthy behaviors for yourself. It could be things like:

- Hurting others or self physically
- Speaking words that belittle others or self
- Repetitive behaviors that hinder healing
- Reclusive tendencies for long periods of time
- Defiance that cannot be reasoned with or redirected
- Obsessive or extreme focus on objects, people, games, or imaginary play
- Shutting down or panicking without ability to move on

For us, it simply looked like imaginative play that was more filled with fear than fun. When I chose reality for my child and led him back to connection with me, only then did we move out of anxiety together. It will look different for every child. You know your child's anxious behaviors best.

Magnetic Words in Action

I got down on the kitchen floor beside my son while he acted like an animal. I began by saying, "I see you," as I mimicked his animal movements and tone. For the first time in a long time his eyes briefly met mine and my heart leaped into my throat. Then I said, "I hear you," and roared like a lion matching his sound. Again, his eyes met mine with a brief side-eye. Then he cried and came closer and let me put my arms around him. I held him as I said, "I'm with you."

I rocked back and forth and began to pray out loud as his trembling body began to relax into mine. The anxiety his little body was holding could not be talked away, corrected away, or magically taken away. It had to be acknowledged (I see and hear you) and cared about (I'm with you). Only then could we begin to move forward.

Looking back, I see this as our first moment of success in moving from chaos to calm. I had tried so many times before to correct him, guide him, and get him to snap out of it. But nothing, I mean absolutely nothing, was working. There are a few reasons why:

- I didn't truly understand anxiety or what motivated my son to act oddly or disengage from reality.
- Sometimes anxiety simply looked like misbehavior.
- I had parented three other children before him and used my pro-parenting tactics that just didn't work for this child. I thought maybe I had lost my touch.

Why things worked now:

- I realized I could not do this in my own strength and I needed God to help me.
- I was willing to try something new and was ready to learn.

- I challenged myself to look deeper than the external behavior.
- I worked toward connection and understanding of anxiety.

It makes me think of the memorable words of Josh McDowell, "Rules without relationship leads to rebellion."[2] While anxiety does not equal rebellion, the rules part sure can get us stuck as parents when trying to guide a child beyond these stressful moments.

When we give up our pride that we are great parents, we begin to shift from *I got this* to *Only God can do this*. This is exactly where I was. *God, please help!* Then and only then was I ready to humble myself to ideas of what I thought would work, to asking God to work.

I applied the words from our therapy session, but the ray of sunshine in this life-changing moment was the prayer and connection to God once my son and I were finally in sync.

Connection with God is the foundational key for parents.

There was something special happening in these moments of connection. This was a tool I started using regularly and in time saw progress that could only be attributed to answered prayers. In any relationship, connection is of great value. Connection with God is the foundational key for parents. Then connection and course correction with the child is essential. In a relationship with a child who sees life through a lens of fear and anxiety, there is often no moving forward until the child is seen and understood—connected.

Many well-meaning parents will continue to struggle parenting an anxious child simply because they do not understand the child's brain chemistry and thought process, or they are not willing to learn a new way of dealing with what is going wrong. Approaches like spanking or time-outs during an anxious episode, raising your voice, removing the child from the situation, taking things away, and avoiding social settings have likely left you exhausted and at a loss. I've been there. Desperate. Depleted. Thinking things would never get better.

I will boldly tell you: You simply cannot parent an anxious child the same way you parent every other child. Every child is different. With that said, your anxious child still needs boundaries (maybe even more rigid ones), training in respect and social cues, and clear instruction and expectations. It does not serve your child or your family well to let your child's anxiety take over your family. Still, it is essential to address how to help a child who has emotions, thoughts, or actions that are out of control due to anxious feelings. And you can do this!

There is a time and place for all of the traditional parenting tools and there is a biblical basis for many of them, but as I navigate my child's anxiety, I am learning the battlefield is best fought on my knees rather than through my know-it-all attitude. I have had to set aside things that worked before because anxiousness isn't just rebellion or back talk. There is so much more going on. I can easily shut down a mouthy child or use my "mom look" and voice to gain control over the situation. But to truly guide my child's anxious heart toward God, I have to address the very real fear in the room. The first step is saying, I see you. I hear you. I'm with you.

I tried the *I see you, I hear you, and I'm with you* script over and over, always ending in a time of asking God to rewire my child's brain. Slowly, my child began to move from less fear toward more confidence and calmness. Your child can experience this shift too!

The world has countless books on the brain and how to combat anxiety. The practice of matching and being attuned to the child's needs to help with anxiety is well known in the mental health world. While the secular world knows this method of connecting with a child, I believe this was originally God's idea. He was the first to see us and our great need for a Savior. He went so far that He sent Jesus to "match" humanity. God literally became like us to heal us.

> For He made Him who knew no sin to be sin for us, that we might become the righteousness of God in Him. (2 CORINTHIANS 5:21)

truth-telling time

As Christians, we believe God's Word holds the truth we need to live as Jesus has called us to live, including parenting. Here are a couple of the tried-and-true verses we often consider when thinking about biblical parenting.

- "Train up a child in the way he should go, and when he is old he will not depart from it." (Proverbs 22:6)
- "Children, obey your parents in the Lord, for this is right. 'Honor your father and mother,' which is the first commandment with promise: 'that it may be well with you and you may live long on the earth.' And you, fathers, do not provoke your children to wrath, but bring them up in the training and admonition of the Lord." (Ephesians 6:1–4)

These verses teach key truths like:

- Parents are to train children in the Lord's ways.
- Children are to honor and obey their parents.
- Parents are not to provoke children to anger.

With these foundational biblical parenting ground rules, we can individually answer to God for how we execute them. I am learning the key in training my children up by not provoking them to anger is to use communication with God as my main parenting tool. He is my go-to resource and source for training all of my children. When I take my children and my parenting to God in prayer, I am asking God to see, hear, and be with me and my children rather than depending on myself.

We see Jesus model this method of seeing, hearing, and being with us in the way He interacts with others. Take a journey through the life of Christ in the Bible and you will find Jesus modeling gentleness, compassion, firmness, and prayer. These are more of those magnetic words that bring together rather than separate, ostracize, or isolate.

If we are to bring up children in the ways of the Lord, taking a look at the way the Lord cared for others is a good place to begin. We find Him speaking the truth, praying, doing miracles, all during His daily routines. Some of the miracles He performed include healing the sick, giving sight to the blind, casting out demons, calming storms, and many more. Each time He performed a miracle, He looked at the person in some way. He often asked what they needed. Then He acted on the need He saw or heard.

He saw them.

He heard them.

He was with them.

Jesus modeled the magnetic connection psychologists now call matching. He is indeed the Creator of all.

> Jesus modeled the magnetic connection psychologists now call matching.

He sees you right where you are, doing your best to parent the child He has given you.

He hears your prayers and the deepest desperation of your heart.

He is with you right now as you wrestle to figure out your next move.

☆ all-star tip

Before we jump into begging God to help our children, we often need to ask God to see, hear, and be with us first. Practice what you will implement with your child by connecting with God.

Remind yourself:

God sees me.

God hears me.

God is with me.

Say it this way: *God, I need Your help. I know You see me down here struggling to parent. I know You hear my desperate cry for help. I know You are with me, but I need You to be ever present right now so I know what to do next. In Jesus' name, amen.*

a ray of sunshine

Dear Jesus, Help me to know that You are God and You are with me always. I know I can trust You even when I am overwhelmed. I pray today that I will remember that You see me, hear me, are with me, and love me. These four things I pray. In Jesus' name, amen.

parent heart check

- If we could sit across the table from each other, sip our coffees, and confess our biggest parenting pain point right now, what would yours be?

- Take those words. That pain. The unknowns. The fear of regret. The struggle that you haven't shared with your friends because they won't understand, and lay it at the feet of the One who saw you first and already hears that ache in your soul for help. He is here right now with you and me. And He is with your child too.

game plan highlights

- Anxiety is not typically a misbehavior as much as it is a misunderstood expression of fear.
- When we give up our pride that we are great parents, we begin to shift from *I got this* to *Only God can do this.*
- Give the child the tools they need to cope before coping is necessary.
- Connection with God is the foundational key for parents.

chapter three

building connection

The eyes are often called the window to the soul. Maybe you have noticed how your child's eyes change in moments of anxious thoughts or spiraling behaviors. There is definitely something to observe and acknowledge by looking deep into a child's eyes in both happy moments and moments of heightened feelings and overwhelm.

In this chapter we will discover how the power of engaging the child's eyes, hands, and ears can empower you and them to move beyond a stressful moment with confidence and success. Buckle up as we begin this chapter with a little bit of the nerdy research when it comes to eyes, hands, and ears. I promise if you take it all in, you'll be attempting the tips in this chapter as soon as possible.

Studies show:

- Eye contact helps with relational bonding.
- Eye contact helps enhance a positive mood.[1]
- Eye contact with faces holding angry expressions affect the brain dramatically in a negative way.
- Eye contact with neutral expressions often evoke feelings of fear.[2]

This makes me consider what my child sees when their eyes meet mine. As parents, we have a great responsibility to consider the child's eyes, both how they appear and how they perceive. Is my face calm, happy, and engaging or igniting an uncertain response in my child without me even realizing it? An anxious child's eyes give parents insight for deeper understanding and regulation.

Hands can also be a telltale sign that something is not right. Hands might fidget, tremble, be clenched tight, or be used to bite nails, pick scabs, pinch, hit, or a number of other things. When fear, anxiety, or frustration is in the mix, hands can often be used for harm. Simple non-harming fidgeting can also drive a parent crazy if they don't understand why a child won't just be still. We want to teach our children that hands are for working, loving, and using to honor God.

Children struggling with anxiety often have overlapping diagnoses or behaviors to consider. Sensory, social, and undiagnosed issues can pile on top of each other, making it challenging for parents to know what they are truly dealing with. Dr. Rotz, author of *Fidget to Focus*, says, "Fidgeting can serve as a coping mechanism for managing anxiety or stress. Individuals with ADHD often experience higher rates of anxiety, and fidgeting

> can provide a way to regulate that stress effectively. Movement can have a calming effect on the brain, reducing anxiety levels and promoting a greater sense of control during challenging tasks."[3]

The final body part we will talk about in this section is the ear. When a child is in the midst of any kind of escalated episode, they are not always hearing things the way they are intended. Their perception is often inhibited by the anxiety. They might hear a slightly raised voice as extreme yelling or translate a stern facial expression as intense anger.

Have you ever given your child instructions firmly only for them to burst into tears saying, "You yelled at me!" Knowing that their senses might not interpret your actions clearly is a key to value and understand. While some children might try to use this as manipulation, anxious children often truly interpret your sternness as yelling.

> We cannot control how a child perceives or hears, but we can control how we offer instruction and guidance.

Sometimes parents do yell or scream. If that is you, just admit it. Even if the child seemed to deserve it, we all know it is not our best parenting moment. I will be the first to raise my hand and say I've raised my voice in moments when I could have handled things with more compassion in my tone. If you feel like yelling is the only way, or it is all you know, I have a different method for you to experiment with. Try singing the words you feel like yelling. It sounds crazy, I know, but you might see some good results. For one, you won't be yelling and it will help you calm down and think about the outcome you really want.

We cannot control how a child perceives or hears, but we can control how we offer instruction and guidance. This simple tool has made some sweet memories for my children in moments that I could have made traumatic through my own potential loss of self-control. One sweet moment was when my toddler stopped in her tracks, looked squarely into my eyes, and sang right back to me. Try it and let me know how it works for you.

We've all read the funny memes that say things like *gentle parenting is for gentle kids and my kids are gangsters*. While we can chuckle under our breath at these sarcastic sayings, we also just about can't breathe in the moments of real chaos that ensue with our children who struggle with bigger feelings than we feel equipped to handle.

Here is the hope: If we can speak Bible truth over the eyes, hands, and ears of our children, asking God to help them see, feel, and hear the way He designed them to, we can see positive results in our children.

Let's unpack how this can work:

1. Work toward eye contact. Eyeball to eyeball is a power play you need in your playbook. Do whatever you can do to practice eye contact daily. Have you ever observed your child looking down, staring off into space, or avoiding eye contact at all costs? When my son was young, eye contact was extremely difficult for him. Even now, I can immediately tell when he is afraid or struggling by his lack of eye contact with another person.

Evaluate if eye contact is hard for your child and work toward practicing little wins daily. A simple way to do this is to ask the child, "Let me see your beautiful eyes."[4] If this is too hard of a command for the child, try, "Can you tell me what color my eyes are?" Both of these ideas give the child an opportunity to look into your eyes. Once you have eye contact, attempt to keep it as long as possible. Repeat this process like a game for younger children. For older kids this might be a bigger challenge as they are already accustomed to looking away. You might have to try more direct speech like, "I need to see your eyes before we can move forward."

Note: Do not move forward in this game plan until eye contact is established if the child is physically and mentally capable of making eye contact.

2. Work toward willing hands. After eye contact is established, the next goal is tender, gentle, predictable physical touch through the hands.[5] It is not grabbing, pulling, pinching, or forcing hands. It is a child willingly giving their hands and placing them in the hands of the caregiver. The parent can use words like, "Give me your hands" while also holding their own hands out in front of them, palms up and hands open.

Why is this step so important?

It models a few behaviors that will help a parent and child connect and gives the child the power to comply rather than force a decision. This is not a battle of wills; it is the way I have decided to help my child succeed. If I force my child, I might get a perceived outcome that I desire. I might even avoid embarrassment and humiliation in the moment. But if I take the extra time to gain my child's undivided attention by guiding them to make the right decision on their own and in their own emotionally calm mental state, that is what I call a true win. We can force an outcome, or we can forge a new pattern of positive behavior.

Once the parent's hands are open and the child has been asked to give their hands, the goal is for the child to place their hands gently into the parent's while maintaining eye contact. Again, this might take lots of practice. Think of it like a game of peek-a-boo or patty-cake. Becky Bailey, author of *I Love You Rituals*, says, "These things are linked to the development of dopamine. The secret ingredients appear to be eye contact, touch, and the bonding these interactions provide."[6]

This is an opportunity for the parent to show loving eyes and to connect on a spiritual and physical level with the child. If the child cannot maintain eye contact, go back to step one and practice some more. If eye contact is good but hands stay disengaged, use this as an opportunity to briefly talk about how we are learning something new together, and it will work best if we hold hands.

If the child will not engage in offering their hands, try connecting with one finger pointer to pointer, one pinky, or by both parties giving a thumbs up. Do what you can to connect with your child. This is the practice of connection amidst correction. Being on the same team with your child is the goal with this truth-talking exercise. It is helping your child find a new way to deal with the feelings that are bombarding them, not about forcing a desired behavior.

By teaching the child a predictable way to deal with their feelings, you are empowering them to become an emotionally stable adult who can take life as it comes. Shutting them down, never talking about their feelings, and avoiding the real problem at hand, the child will continue to struggle, and the parent will end up wondering what went wrong.

Once you have connected the eyes and the hands of an emotionally struggling child, you have won a battle many only wish to accomplish. To calmly get to this point it is going to take practice and hard work on both the parent and the child's part. It might take multiple tries, sessions, or redos. Don't give up! With practice, this can become a game changer for your family.

3. Speak the truth with your child. Eye to eye and hand to hand—ears are open. Say to the child, "I can see you are afraid of ________ [fill in the blank naming the child's fear]. Sometimes there are things that make us feel afraid. It is normal to have feelings of fear, but God gives us power to help us with those feelings. Let's pray right now and ask for His help."

Example Prayer: Dear God, Sometimes fear is really big and scary. Help us right now to focus on what is true. You give us power. You love us. You want our minds and bodies to be under control and calm. Help our eyes to see each other with love. Help our hands to hold each other gently. Help our minds to rest in Your power and not get out of control. In Jesus' name, amen.

Here are some things you can discuss with your child about eyes, hands, and ears during a calm moment:

Eyes: Say, "What color are your eyes? What color are mine?" Blink your eyes together. Try to wink. Have a staring contest. Read Dr. Seuss's *Eye Book* or look up eyes online and see all the different colors and shapes. Now practice connecting eye to eye. Tell your child you are going to practice. Say, "Give me your eyes." Encourage your child to look at your eyes as soon as they hear the words. See how fast they can do it. Keep it fun. Make it a game but make the fun part the eye contact not the looking away part.

Hands: Say, "What can we use our hands for?" Discuss how we can use them for work and play, but not for hurting, hitting, or destroying things. Lean into this activity by focusing on the power of love God has given us and the ability we have to give hugs, hold hands, and encourage each other with a gentle pat on the back, high five, or thumbs-up. Practice these with your child and work on your eye-to-eye, hand-to-hand connection in a calm moment. If your child is always tearing things up, picking scabs, biting nails, or tapping, they might be a sensory seeker. To fill a sensory seeker's needs, try giving them one of these for ten minutes before you attempt hand to hand: play-dough, a tub full of dry rice or beans, a fidget spinner, drawing pad, or any other activity that will make them use their hands.

Ears: Try speaking in different voices and volumes and make it a game. Whisper, squeak, speak low, speak high-pitched. Have your child repeat your voice. My favorite to use is a whisper or a singing voice. The goal here is to continue connecting and letting your child learn to listen to your words while eyes and hands are connected to yours. Ask them how they feel when you speak in each tone. Have them ask you. Talk about the respectful way to talk to each other and what is acceptable in your home.

truth-telling time

For God has not given us a spirit of fear, but of power and of love and of a sound mind.

(2 TIMOTHY 1:7)

Fear is a response that doesn't have to be taught. It is a natural instinct that we see in infants right out of the womb. The flailing arms and little hands that open wide searching to find a home in the free space of the cold air ignites a feeling of insecurity in a tiny human being. As the child grows, these feelings of insecurity, fear, panic, or unknown can grow too. But so can security and connection.

If little eyes can gaze into the eyes of a mother or father and connect, security is fed. If tiny hands can grasp hold of an adult's finger, they find calm and safety. If little ears hear the soothing sound of the familiar voices they've heard from the beginning, they grow in confidence knowing everything will be okay. This feeling of security works wonders in a developing mind to grow the power and practice of self-control.

Learning to see, feel, and hear the good gifts of security God has given us offers parents and children an opportunity to connect and build on a foundation toward more peaceful situations. Teaching emotional strengthening skills and speaking truth over a child's eyes, hands, and ears empowers both you as the parent and your child to connect in a beautiful way to move from conflict, fighting, or shutdown to calm and connected. It's a parent seeing, hearing, and being with a child and the child in return seeing, hearing, and responding appropriately to the parents' instruction in a stressful situation.

Learning to see, feel, and hear the good gifts of security God has given us offers parents and children an opportunity to connect and build on a foundation toward more peaceful situations.

☆ all-star tip

Use your hands to point to your eyes while you say, "Give me your eyes," and then smoothly move your hands down and open in front of you with palms up saying, "Give me your hands." This physical cue can be used without words once a child learns the game plan. In a moment of high pressure, you can simply point to your eyes and open your hands and your child can respond to your truth telling if you've practiced repeatedly.

a ray of sunshine

Heavenly Father, Lord sometimes things seem scary. Please help me to know I am safe even when things are tough. When I can't see You, please help me to know You are still there. Help me to remember You are omnipotent, omniscient, and omnipresent. In Your One and Holy Name, amen.

parent heart check

- Which one is most difficult for your child: Eyes, Hands, Ears?
- Think of one thing your child is good at when it comes to Eyes, Hands, or Ears.
- When will you talk to your child about Eyes, Hands, Ears?
- Can you see how this method could potentially work for you and your child? What time of day can you implement practicing this game plan? Choose a time and repeat it for several days in a row until it comes easy for you and your child.
- Take time to write in your journal or speak a prayer of gratitude for God giving us the power to have self-control. If this is a big struggle for you or your child and the eyes, hands, and ears idea feels impossible, use this moment to ask God for help to show you how you can best help yourself and your child succeed in these areas.

game plan highlights

- As parents we have a great responsibility to consider the child's eyes, especially an anxious child's eyes as a tool for deeper understanding and regulation.
- We cannot control how a child perceives or hears, but we can control how we offer instruction and guidance.
- Learning to see, feel, and hear the good gifts of security God has given us offers parents and children an opportunity to connect and build on a foundation toward more peaceful situations.

chapter four

moving memories

I pushed the pedals harder with each turn. The wind on my face gave me that exhilarating feeling of freedom you can only get in the wide-open air. Riding a bike as a little girl gave me a sense of collected calmness I can't really even put into words. It's one of my favorite childhood memories. My youngest child is currently learning to ride a bike. The look on her face tells me she is experiencing the same sense of calm I felt as a child. Almost every day she finds her bike and rides around and around and around the driveway until it's time to come inside.

For one of my other children, riding a bike hasn't come as easily. If I challenged them to find an activity that makes them feel free and calm, riding a bike might be the last thing they would choose.

When I hear the words, "It's just like riding a bike," I am reminded riding a bike is a learned activity. It takes balance, practice, and sometimes training wheels. Mom, Dad, the favorite aunt, oldest sibling, or the friend down the street runs behind the wobbly learner while holding on to the seat for dear life hoping for no crashes or skinned knees.

Just like riding a bike doesn't come easy for everyone, the ability to fight fears doesn't either. It will take practice and repeated memorable moments to get things moving in the right direction for both you and your child. Be patient as you both learn how to work toward calm. It might not be just like riding a bike.

Fight, *flight*, or *freeze*. These are well known words in the world of anxious people. It's that response that happens in the brain and body when something feels or seems threatening. Maybe you've experienced this yourself or seen this response in your child. It's that overwhelming sense in the body that makes a person go on immediate physical defense through fighting back, running away, or completely shutting down.

There is a scientific reason this happens:

> During a fight-flight-or-freeze stress response, your adrenal glands pump out a hormone called adrenaline. The surge of adrenaline makes your heart pound, breathing quicken, and muscles tense. Extra oxygen shuttled to your brain makes you super alert and sharpens senses like sight and hearing. Blood sugar and fat spill into the bloodstream to help give you a burst of energy to physically respond.[1]

It can be complicated to know how to respond to a child who struggles with fight, flight, or freeze. When you never know when the stress response will be triggered, it can be challenging to respond in the moment. Some of my best efforts of comforting my child have resulted in a child fighting harder and harder only to end in a complete meltdown by me and the child.

We all deal with fight, flight, or freeze to some degree. Knowing this, I have learned it's best if I give my child opportunities to exercise those fight, flight, and freeze muscles in moments when harm is not around. It's finding moments to use the body to let stress out when the stress is not being obviously seen. It's when the child is not running away, not fighting, and not freezing that I can offer my child the valuable gift of movement memories. In this chapter I want to explore the idea that you can create new memories in response to your child's fears. These new memories include movement of the body.

In his book *Raising Emotionally Strong Boys*, David Thomas shares how participation in physical activities is foundational for helping children through big feelings. He encourages parents to help their child create a list of physical activities. Things like running laps around the yard, doing push-ups, using a boxing bag, punching a pillow, walking the dog, or any other movement activity that will allow the stress that is pent up to get out.[2]

For my son, jumping on the trampoline and doing push-ups are both simple, quick ways to help him regulate his emotions no matter if the emotions are positive or negative. In using his body and getting movement out, the stress response is less severe. He still has his fears and anxieties still hit, but they don't hit him quite as hard if we have been intentional about getting his body moving. I see the same response in my daughter who loves her bike. If she rides her bike until her heart feels free, the response to stressors during that time period are not as explosive. According to some studies, regular exercise works as well as medication for some people to reduce symptoms of anxiety and depression, and the effects can be long-lasting.[3]

For some children, playing a musical instrument is the movement that helps relieve stress so the body can get the overwhelming rush of feelings out. For others, it is swinging on the swing set. The breeze of the wind on the face and the pumping of the legs to go higher is exactly what the body needs rather than using the body in a negative way to push, hit, shove, freeze or run somewhere prohibited by Mom and Dad.

> Regular exercise works as well as medication for some people to reduce symptoms of anxiety and depression, and the effects can be long-lasting.

We all want the same thing: for our children to be okay. And I really believe your child can be. Making movement a part of your child's life is a gift you can give them. Choose an activity you know they enjoy. Do not make this more stressful for them or for you by compounding the anxious feelings and behaviors. If your child can't even do a push-up, do not choose push-ups as their moving activity.

You can find what your child enjoys most and what truly helps them by watching and observing their actions.

- What is their go-to activity?
- What movements do they delight in?
- What gives them that wild and free look on their face without a worry in the world?

In our culture, screens often replace movement and coping strategies. Let me wave a big red flag right here and let's sit down and chat for just a few minutes.

In Jonathan Haidt's bestselling book, *The Anxious Generation*, he proves anxiety is the primary mental health struggle in our younger generation due to an uptick in accessibility to screens.[4] Your child is not alone in their struggle, and you are not alone in your efforts to offer help.

Screens will only extend the inevitable. If you give your child a screen of any kind to "help" them not be anxious, when they are done with the screen, the anxiety that was there before will still be there and might even be worse. Screens might make them sit still, but they do not instill the capability of coping in a healthy way.

We want to give our children the confidence that they are capable of coping without a screen and without Mom or Dad coaching them because eventually they can be. Screens can be educational and entertaining and there is a place and time for them, but screens cannot be our go-to coping strategy if we want our children to use their bodies to honor God. I am not saying throw the iPad away, but to use it wisely rather than as an accessory your child cannot live without. Screens cannot help children truly cope, but God can.

Screens cannot help children truly cope, but God can.

How to implement "moving memories" into your everyday life:

Observe your child during a free playtime outdoors. Find an activity they gravitate to and often desire to do.

Plan a time when you will give them full access to the activity. Make it an enjoyable time with no fear. Make it fun. Make it last.

Speak the truth over them. This is your chance to deposit confidence and coping skills. If you tell them how good they are at an activity, they will want to do that activity more often. Discuss how this activity makes them feel.

Pray and thank God for the ability and opportunity to use their bodies to glorify God. By pointing back to God and reminding them the reason they can move, they will be building spiritual coping skills in the calm moment.

☑ Finish up by teaching them that this activity is something that helps them feel calm and energized. Next time they have an anxious episode, talk about their coping moving activity and give them the opportunity to choose coping over chaos. You might need to choose it for them to begin with. And you might need to find your own way to cope too. Parenting an anxious child is challenging in unique ways and requires unique approaches in helping yourself and your child.

Anxiety often feels too big to handle. Teaching your child, boys and girls, to find what physical activity they can do to get back to baseline will give them a coping skill that can last a lifetime. One study revealed that often people with anxiety were more sedentary. The conclusion was that "when it comes to anxiety, the more exercise the better."[5]

This is a practice we have chosen to use when we are at home that greatly impacts our family dynamics. We use this most when we know routines will be changed for the day or chaos seems to be setting in. We've seen this work with the craziness of holidays, out-of-town guests visiting, and things like snow days when the routine of everything normal is out the window. When I passionately say "Everyone outside!" the kids know that is their cue to find an activity. Some need more specific prompting, but most know that is the prompt that means "Go ride your bike," "Hop on the swings," or "Go play the piano." It's the "find something active to do or Mom will find something for you" prompt. This is a tool we can turn to when spiraling out of control is the only other option for me or a child. This is about giving your child the physical ability to deal with the big emotions inside them. And it gives you the space you need to breathe deeply and care for your own mental health.

truth-telling time

For you were bought at a price; therefore glorify God
in your body and in your spirit,
which are God's.

(1 CORINTHIANS 6:20)

Now that each of my children knows their anxiety-releasing activity, it is not a negative experience to do push-ups, take a few laps, or play an instrument. It becomes a beautiful gift from God and a coping exercise that they can do whenever they need to.

Rather than telling a child to "go find something to do, or I'm going to give you something," now they choose their go-to anxiety fighting activity. It is a gift to them and to our entire family. They learn to put in the effort first. They often choose the activity because they know and have learned how it helps them feel better. This is teaching them to appreciate the reality that God made their bodies move. In purposeful movement, children learn to use the body to honor God and fight anxiety.

"God made our bodies to be healthier and happier when they move. Moving limbs increases heart rate and helps to circulate blood, moving hormones and nutrients through the body to where they need to be—including the brain—for optimal physical, mental, and emotional health."[6] This is the end goal we want our children to land on: "With God's help, you, my dear child, can cope and control yourself even when you are nervous, afraid, or cautious. Because God can and will help you. So let's get moving!"

☆ all-star tip

Make movement a memorable time together. Jump on the trampoline with your child. Swing next to them on the swings. Play catch. Take turns punching a punching bag. Jump rope. Play music and dance together. If you can make memories together while moving, not only are you offering your child a coping strategy for life, you are also connecting with them through love in action.

a ray of sunshine

Dear Lord, I need You today. Help me to use my body to honor You. Help me to not hit or push. Help me to be kind even when it is hard because I know that You are with me in everything. You are with me in the good and the bad. In Jesus' name, amen.

parent heart check

"Exercise isn't just good for your physical health. It's also a great stress reducer as well as an energy booster. Regular aerobic exercise helps the body's "stress system"—mainly parts of the brain and the adrenal glands—release fewer stress hormones in response to daily stressors. At the same time, exercise stimulates endorphin production, creating a calming, mood-lifting effect that can make it easier to cope with stress."[7]

- What is one activity with movement that you know your child enjoys?
- What time of day works best for your family to encourage your child to move through this activity?

- Are screens a struggle for you and your child? Plan a no screen time of day and replace it with movement instead. What time of day could you implement this idea?
- Write in your journal or say a prayer thanking God for the ability you and your child have to make memories through activities that make you move. After all, your arms, legs, hands and feet are a gift from God, so thank Him for them together.

> If you can make memories while moving, not only are you offering your child a coping strategy for life, you are also connecting with them through love in action.

game plan highlights

- Making movement a part of your child's life is a gift you can give them.
- Screens might make them sit still, but they do not instill the capability of coping in a healthy way.
- In purposeful movement, children learn to use the body to honor God and fight anxiety.

Weekly Prayer Guide for My Child's Body from Head to Toe

For a printable version of the prayer guides in this book go to MicahMaddox.com.

Instructions: Use the prayer guide below by praying the prayers provided or create your own.

Sunday: My Child's Brain

God, please help my child's brain to function in the way You created it. Please heal the pathways that struggle to connect and rewire the parts that need support. Give me wisdom to see how I can best support and guide them. In Jesus' name, amen.

Monday: My Child's Eyes

God, please help my child's eyes. Protect them from seeing things that would lead them to sin and pain. Help them use their eyes to look for You in all things. Please make Yourself known to them so they can see Your goodness. In Jesus' name, amen.

Tuesday: My Child's Ears

God, please help my child's ears to hear exactly what You want them to hear. When they struggle to listen, open their ears to my voice and to the voice of the other adults in their life who love and lead them. Give them ears to hear Your voice and listen more than they speak. In Jesus' name, amen.

Wednesday: My Child's Mouth

God, please help my child to control their mouth. Give them wisdom to be quiet when it is time and to speak up when necessary. Give them boldness to speak truth. When they don't know what to do, help them to lift their voice in prayer to You. In Jesus' name, amen.

Thursday: My Child's Heart

God, please work in my child's heart. I pray they will develop a personal heart relationship with You. Help them to have motives that honor You. Guide and protect their heart as they face this world today. In Jesus' name, amen.

Friday: My Child's Hands

God, please help my child to use their hands to love others well. Please help them to control their impulses of aggression, anger, or fear. Give them a desire to want to serve others. In Jesus' name, amen.

Saturday: My Child's Feet

God, please help my child to go where You want them to go. Guide their steps. When they get off track please pull them back to You. Help me to see where I need to step in and where I need to step back. In Jesus' name, amen.

Activities for Parents & Children

For short videos and printable activity pages visit MicahMaddox.com

Activity 1: Seeking Calm

Instructions: Read this poem to your child and talk about how to stop, breathe, and think. Use the steps and hand motions in chapter 1 to discuss what it means to stop, breathe, and think and then practice.

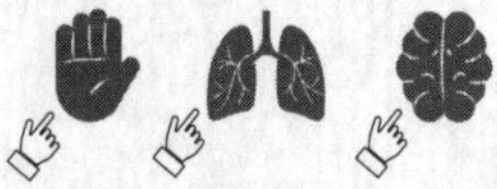

Stop. Breathe. Think.

The world moves fast
Things pass by
Trees and grass
Clouds and sky

But I can stop in all the rush
I can tell my brain to hush

Breathe in
Breathe out
Slow and steady
I can breathe until I'm ready

All is still and calm right now
I can think
I know how

Stopping
Breathing
Thinking too
This game is fun to play with you

Activity 2: Magnetic Words

Instructions: Go through these steps with your child. Then practice connecting through *I see you. I hear you. I'm with you.*

1. Go outside and look around.
2. Choose something you see that you like. Talk about it.
3. Now listen.
4. Ask: What do you hear?
5. Ask: Who is with you?
6. Take a few minutes to walk around outside together looking for different things you can see and hear.
7. Go inside and both parent and child draw a picture of what you saw and heard together.
8. Talk about no matter where we go, even if we can't be together, God is always with us.

Activity 3: Building Connection

Instructions: Read this poem to your child. Talk about each body part and how we can use them properly. Use the questions in chapter 3 to prompt the conversation. I've provided a few quick conversation starters for you.

Eyes, Hands, Ears

I use my eyes every day
They help me work
They help me play
I see the stars in dark of night
I see the birds in air in flight

I use my hands most all the time
I clap clap clap
Point, snap snap snap
My hands can draw and paint and scribble
I can use my hands to dribble

I use my ears to hear birds sing
I hear music and the phone ring
Voices sound different
Some soft some loud
When I listen I feel proud

Conversation Prompts

Eyes: Conversation Starter

"What color are your eyes? What color are mine? Can you wink?" Play the staring game. See how long your child can maintain eye contact. Keep it light and fun.

Hands: Conversation Starter

"What is something you like to do with your hands?" Ideas: Play with play-dough, build something, plant flowers, color, paint, Legos, throw a ball, pet a dog. . . . Talk about how we use our hands to love not hurt. As the child communicates about hands, give high fives as they participate well.

Ears: Conversation Starter

"Can you copy my sound? Make fun sounds with your voice. Some loud. Some soft." The goal here is to continue connecting with your child. Now switch and let them make the noises first while you listen to repeat the sounds. Work on eye contact while you make the sounds.

Activity 4: Moving Memories

Instructions: Have your child make a list or draw five activities they like to do that involve movement. The activities are not limited to outdoors. It can be any activity that moves any part of the body.

1.

2.

3.

4.

5.

Ideas for activities:

- Running
- Skipping
- Jumping jacks
- Push-ups
- Jumping rope
- Make an obstacle course
- Hopscotch
- Patty-cake
- Swinging
- Skating
- Scooter
- Swimming
- Dribbling a basketball
- Kicking a soccer ball
- Playing catch
- Jumping on a trampoline
- Dancing
- Working with a parent—anything that involves movement. It could be as simple as baking or as intense as chopping wood.
- Working out
- Play-dough

- Building Legos
- Stacking blocks
- Coloring
- Painting
- Sidewalk chalk
- Chasing bubbles
- Practicing a musical instrument

Note: The activity does not have to be extreme or even use the entire body. The only requirement is movement of the body in some way. Scrolling or tapping a screen does not count.

After the list is made, choose one activity to do together today. Then have your child choose which activity they will do the next time they begin to feel anxious. Print the list from my website for quick reference.

part two

game plan for calming the mind

chapter five

learning what-is statements

The greatest spiritual battle of our generation is fought between our ears.[1]

I sat on the edge of my child's bed and firmly placed my hands on his scalp. With his bristled black hair coiled beneath my fingertips, I begged God to heal the pathways in his mind.

Night after night, I repeated the practice. One or two hands pressing into the dark black coils pleading with God for his mind. Most nights I would pray with tears. Sometimes with deep fear tucked between my words. The unknowns of how he could move beyond his fears filled me with fear too. It all just seemed like too much, like maybe he would never be free from the fears and anxieties that he wrestled with day after day.

After several nights of praying, there we sat again together. I said amen. He opened his deep dark eyes, looked into mine, and asked,

"Mom, can I pray?" I swallowed hard and tried to hold back the tears. "Yes." We closed our eyes again and bowed our heads. His words filled the room. Time seemed to pause. I held on to every word until he said amen. I almost don't have words to describe the feeling of hearing him ask God to help him with his fears and mind.

While I know God is the one who can help him, when He actually did, I was surprised. Paul says it plainly in Philippians 4:7, "And the peace of God, which surpasses all understanding, will guard your hearts and minds through Christ Jesus" (ESV).

Why do we doubt what God says He can do?

The goal of this book is to help you as a parent realize with consistent guidance, prayer, modeling, and asking God, your child can learn how to go to God for peace for themselves. I've seen and experienced it for myself and for my child. I get a front-row seat to watch my children seek God for help even when it is difficult. It is not always neat and tidy, but it is progress. The growth is undeniable. You and your child can experience it too.

It can sound kind of churchy or trite to say "Just pray for your child." But in this chapter, I want to encourage you to set aside the efforts of all the right words. The right tone. The right script. Get with your child and cry out to God on their behalf. Let them hear you ask God for help for them. Name their fears and beg God to help.

The world's ways of dealing with anxiety will work to a degree, but divine intervention is something the world cannot help you work through. The psychology experts say millions of people struggle with anxious thoughts.[2] While this might comfort us to know we are not alone, it doesn't change anything except giving us a little comfort to know our children are not the only ones.

We cannot expect change if we are relying on ourselves or on the world's ways. Peace does not come aside from God. Peace only comes inside because of God. The mind is a complex place. It asks questions, develops answers, and sends signals to every part of the body. The Bible speaks much of the mind and the power of God over it.

> Peace does not come aside from God. Peace only comes inside because of God.

We do not have to settle for the idea or belief that this is just the way things will always be. God can change it. He is able! For some, there are diagnoses that won't be changed, but that does not mean behaviors, responses, and peace cannot be altered and achieved. God offers peace to all. In the next few chapters, we are going to unpack what the Bible says about how God changes the pathways of the mind.

In his book *Anxious for Nothing*, bestselling author Max Lucado says, "Anxiety is a meteor shower of what-ifs."[3] I love the word picture of a meteor shower. It is uncontrollable and unpredictable. When we live with what-ifs as our go-to thought process, we forget what God can do for and in our child's life. Instead of letting anxiety rule with what-ifs in your mind about your child's struggles, I want to encourage you to focus on and pray *what is*. What I mean is changing your narrative and words about your child and about God. Defining who God is and what God does will work wonders in shifting the mindset from fear to faith in God for you and your child.

- Do not pray, "God, what is wrong with my child or what is wrong with me?"
- Instead, pray something like, "God, You created my child. And You do not make mistakes. I know You will help us."
- Take it a step further and pray, "God, You are the Good Shepherd. I know You will give me direction and guidance to help my child in this difficult moment."

This simple change empowers us as parents to shift our mindset from anxiety to certainty. It is the transformation of worry to wisdom. God is in control! He holds each of us in the palm of His hand. He knows your child better than you do. *Lord, I trust You* prayers will do more to strengthen your heart than *Lord, I can't take this* prayers. By focusing on *who God is* in our situation with our anxious child it will change our mindset and shift our hearts toward truth and hope.

Let's practice applying this mindset shift.

- Think about what is. Do not allow yourself to ask any what-if questions about your child or your parenting in this moment.
- Pray about what is. Tell God what is true. Some of these what-is statements might have a negative slant such as *my child is anxious*, but in this exercise let's look for positive what-is statements.
- God is good.
- Life is beautiful.
- My child is a gift from God.
- Calmness is possible.
- God is able to change things.
- God is my strength.
- God is my refuge.
- God is my help and hope.

In using what-is statements, we can shift our mindset. We have the capability to alter the momentum and change the way we parent. No more what-ifs. Focus on what is. Even if it means saying, *This is hard*. It is okay to speak honestly about what is, but God's word is clear it is not okay to continue wallowing in anxiety. Instead, Paul is clear in his instruction to pray instead.

This might look like a bedtime prayer with hands on your child's head like I described earlier, or it could be praying in the school drop-off or pick-up line at school. It might be prayer around your kitchen table. Or prayer as you sit in the sandbox with your little one. It could be as you take a walk with your growing preteen. The time or place does not matter. It only matters that it happens and it happens regularly.

> In using what-is statements, we can shift our mindset.

truth-telling time

For today let's lay the groundwork of praying for our children's minds by taking one step from Philippians 4:6: "Be anxious for nothing, but in everything by prayer and supplication, with thanksgiving, let your requests be made known to God."

When the Bible says don't be anxious about anything, that alone can feel like an impossible suggestion. But I don't think Paul was merely suggesting. He was instructing the church. His message to believers was to stop worrying and to start praying. Paul gave the church an anecdote for the troubles they felt and experienced. The trouble was called anxiety. The anecdote was prayer. Paul said the result was peace beyond understanding. Why do we wrestle so much to believe our children can experience the same peace?

For us, bedtime is the sweet spot for our anxiety-battling prayers. Maybe because we've experienced utter chaos at bedtime so many times. It's when all the "I needs" come out.

I need a drink.

I need a Band-Aid.

I need to potty.

I need to tell you something.

I need a snack.

Mommy, I need you.

We've fought hard to find peace at bedtime. We go potty. Get one last drink. Make sure bellies are full. Comfort all the boo-boos. And talk about the day. There's finally a calm that sets in during the bedtime routine that prepares my own heart and my child's heart. We read a few books and sing a few songs. Then we pray. No special script. No special words. Just *what-is* words flowing from the heart up to heaven. No *what-ifs* or *I needs* allowed once all needs are met. Sweet dreams. A goodnight prayer. I'll see you in the morning. We still have challenging moments at times, but we know how to aim for *what is* over *what if* with God's help through prayer.

Children do not need to see a perfect parent, they just need a praying parent.

☆ all-star tip

Use this prayer time to pray for your own fears and your child's fears. Let them hear you vulnerably share that you also struggle. Children do not need to see a perfect parent, they just need a praying parent. Talk to your child about what-is statements. Use them in your bedtime prayer tonight. Here are some examples of questions you can ask.

Questions to ask your child:

1. What is true about your day today?
2. What is true about you?
3. What is true about God?

Follow these questions with a prayer including each answer you and your child came up with.

a ray of sunshine

Dear Jesus, I need You today. Help me to focus on what is true. I need You to help me focus on You because You are the Lord of Lords. You are the King of kings. You are the Prince of Peace. I need that peace today. In Jesus' name, amen.

parent heart check

Take time to write in your journal or think about your what-ifs. Let's go ahead and get them out so you don't have to say them anymore. You might have more than three, but think through your top three what-ifs when it comes to parenting your child.

- What if . . .
- What if . . .
- What if . . .

Now take a moment to write in your journal or think about a couple of what-is statements. I have provided prompts to help get you started.

- My child is . . .
- My God is . . .
- Say or write a prayer in your journal using the *what-is* statements you came up with.

game plan highlights

- Peace does not come aside from God. Peace only comes inside because of God.
- In using what-is statements, we can shift the mindset.
- We cannot expect change if we are relying on ourselves.
- Children do not need to see a perfect parent, they just need a praying parent.

chapter six

practicing gratitude

"Why do people die?"

"How do the babies get out of the mommies' bellies?"

"Why do they look like that?"

"How long do you think I will live?"

These are real questions my kids have asked me. And it is usually when we are driving somewhere and the questions seem to come from out of nowhere. I'm sure you could write your own list of your child's questions.

A child's questions give us a little insight into their growing minds. The mind is filled with ideas, questions, narratives, emotions, beliefs, and dreams. Sometimes we totally get what they are thinking by what they say or do, and other times it seems like they are on another planet.

For an anxious child, questions often turn into statements that can look more like this:

- *I never get a turn.* Rather than, "When is it my turn?" anxious kids seem to jump straight to the statement that they will never get a turn and they struggle to wait their turn.
- *No one ever listens to me.* When they can't seem to get their way, they begin to conclude no one wants to hear what they have to say. Rather than asking, "Can I tell you something?" they tend to land on a false idea that no one cares about what they have to say.
- *They hate me.* When they lose a game or can't seem to get approval, they begin to think the person who seems to be causing the loss must not like them. so that is why they are causing them to lose the game.
- *I can't do it.* When success isn't happening quickly enough for the child, they begin to lean into the idea that they are not capable of succeeding at whatever they are trying to do. It could be simple like pouring a bowl of cereal, or more complicated like finishing a homework assignment. But regardless, their perception impacts their actions. Rather than asking how to do it, or seeking help, they might give up prematurely simply due to fear of failure or embarrassment.

While you might look at these and consider them plain old negative self-talk, this is the very real narrative kids with anxiety tell themselves over and over. They often have absolutes specific to them that they cannot seem to kick. It is a way of thinking they have practiced and now has grown until it is controlling the everyday actions or lack of actions due to fear. Kids dealing with anxiety often are preoccupied by what might go wrong.[1]

I'm never going to win seemed to be the go-to narrative for my son. Team sports proved to be a challenge. When he got placed on a team that couldn't score, that statement he already focused on began to become engraved in his mind. But it didn't just sit there in his little mind during game time, it went home with him after every game.

"Why am I such a loser?"

The truth was he was on a team and teams win and lose together. It is not one person who lost, but the entire team lost together. Rewriting this narrative in a different way had the potential to reframe his thoughts. But it also took work and guidance.

The struggle usually comes because we as parents do this too. We tell ourselves a narrative that isn't true or is half-truths tucked in insecurity.

- "I am failing as a parent."
- "I can't get it together like her."
- "Why do I seem to be the only mom in the entire congregation struggling right now?"
- "Why is my kid the one who always gets singled out?"

There is one practice we have found that works wonders in combating the negative narrative and questions for both my child and myself. It is the practice of gratitude. Rather than asking the negative questions, we replace them with statements of thanksgiving. This is something everyone can do. There is no fear of failure for this task because we are all capable of being thankful. Even the most anxious child can work on thinking about something they are thankful for.

Even the most anxious child can work on thinking about something they are thankful for.

We can apply this daily as many times as necessary until we get the desired result—calmness and confidence.

Supplies to gather:

1. A notebook—either surprise your child with one or let them go to the store to pick one up. Call it "My Gratitude Journal." You can also find a Gratitude Guide on my website, MicahMaddox.com, and look at the end of this section in the activities section for a little gratitude practice to do with your child.

2. Pens, pencils, or markers—either surprise them or let your child choose their favorites.

Gratitude Process

TIME: Choose a time of day when you can do this regularly. This is especially important if your child is in an anxiety rut. If they are struggling daily, do this exercise daily. The earlier in the day, the better to get them started on the right track.

PLACE: Choose a place. Make it as routine as possible. Choose a specific seat at the table or counter. Go outside. Or let them grab a soft pillow and blanket or pile on your bed as a special treat.

AMBIANCE: Make this time enjoyable. This should not be like punishment or correction. This is a time of gratitude that is kind of like preventive medicine. When the mind thinks about good things, the brain and body feels better. If the child isn't wanting to participate or is not capable, make it as easy as possible and just do it verbally this time. Try for a written experience another day.

ROUTINE: Write or draw ten things you are thankful for. Do this with your child. You make your own list and make sure your child is on the list. Let them hear you say how grateful you are for them. Do not make it behavior based, meaning do not put on your list, "I am thankful Johnny obeyed Mommy today," or "I am thankful Suzie didn't have a meltdown today." Simply show gratitude for who they are, not what they have done or not done.

This practice of gratitude is laying the foundation for a lifetime of worshiping God. When we think about what we are thankful for, we are less likely to create negative absolutes in our thought process.

Let's take it a little bit deeper. Not only can you make a gratitude list, but the next step is writing letters of gratitude.

The practice of gratitude is laying the foundation for a lifetime of worshiping God and serving others.

One study conducted at Berkeley had a group of college students write letters of gratitude over four weeks and then over twelve weeks. The reports were undeniable. Those who wrote the letters had significant improvement in their mental health at the four-week mark and the twelve-week mark. It was like a snowball effect on the brain. The uniqueness of this study was that the participants were all people who were currently seeking professional psychological counseling, so they were to some degree concerned about their mental health. One of the main reasons the gratitude letters worked so well to improve the mental health of the letter writers was that it focused the mind on the positive things others had done for them. This way of thinking consumed the mind so much that it struggled to focus on negative thoughts. The conclusion of the study was, "Gratitude reverses our priorities to help us appreciate the people and things we do."[2]

If your child struggles with overwhelming negative thoughts, fears, or emotions, have them try writing letters of gratitude. You can have your child narrate them and you can type them and print them out for them to color on. Or if your child is capable, have them write a good old-fashioned thank-you note. This is not so much about thank-you notes for special gifts, although thank-you notes are sweet for those. Think a little deeper with me. Help your child come up with people who have blessed their life in some way such as:

- By a simple act of kindness
- A word of encouragement
- A service they provide to the community

People who you might consider:

- Grandparents or family members
- Teachers or leaders at church or school
- Special friends
- Community leaders
- First responders

Make a list with your child and begin writing letters of gratitude. The study showed after just a few weeks there can be dramatic improvement in the brain. Gratitude is a simple way to begin shifting the thought patterns from negative to positive. The beautiful part is that while neuroscience proves it, God's Word designed it.

truth-telling time

Paul gives us the instructions for gratitude clearly in Philippians 4:6: "Be anxious for nothing, but in everything by prayer and supplication, with thanksgiving, let your requests be made known to God."

Not only do we need to pray like we discussed in chapter 5, but in that praying spirit there is a key to relief from anxious thinking—Paul calls it *thanksgiving*.

I like to think of it as *practicing gratitude*. This simple yet profound action is not something you receive or experience. It is a choice to look at life with a mind of thankfulness. It is a practice of learning to be grateful in getting a win or going through a loss. It is choosing thankfulness rather than thinking it over.

It takes a little time. It takes a couple of supplies and intentional thinking. But the results will last a lifetime for both you and your child.

Anticipate the moments your child struggles most. If it is before a ball game or big test, that is the time to make a gratitude list or write your letters of gratitude. Use this time to build up your child. Create a gratitude list about your child and about God. Share it with your child and pray with your child thanking God for the things on your list.

If you can use your gratitude prayers prior to a stressful moment, you can reference it if things go off the rails. Remind your child, "We are going to focus on what we can see that is good." It is not about never noticing the negative, it's about offering an alternative perspective. It is choosing the glass half full rather than half empty.

Challenge your child to write their own gratitude list or write their own letter of gratitude.

☆ all-star tip

Play the Gratitude Game in the car. This requires zero supplies and your child will be asking to play on the next car trip. When you get into the car and everyone is buckled, tell your child or children you are going to play the Gratitude Game. You choose who gets to go first. Each player names one thing they are thankful for. Keep going until everyone in the car gets a turn. Repeat. Play until you get to your destination. After all, gratitude holds the power to shift the anxious brain toward calmness.

a ray of sunshine

Lord, thank You for everything You have done for me. Thank You for my mom. Thank You for my dad. Thank You for my sisters and brother. Thank You for clothes on my back. Thank You for shoes on my feet. I want to say thank You for everything. Great are You, Lord! In Jesus' name, amen.

parent heart check

Do you tell yourself negative statements? Which one of these do you tell yourself the most?

- I feel like I'm failing.
- I can't do it all.
- I'm going to lose it.

Think about other repetitive negative thought statements you tell yourself about your parenting and write them in your journal.

Consider practicing gratitude right now by making your own gratitude list in your journal. Slow down and think intentionally about your list. Name at least five things.

Evaluate how you feel after making your list.

When will you sit down and guide your child to write or draw a gratitude list of their own or create letters of gratitude?

Identify two to three activities or times of day that tend to be a struggle for your child. Write them in your journal.

Use the times of day you wrote down to practice gratitude with your child. Have them make a daily list at the same time every day or choose one person to write a letter of gratitude to each day.

Take a moment to write or say a prayer using your gratitude list.

game plan highlights

- Even the most anxious child can work on thinking about something they are thankful for.
- This practice of gratitude is laying the foundation for a lifetime of worshiping God.
- Gratitude is a simple way to begin shifting the thought patterns from negative to positive. The beautiful part is that while neuroscience proves it, God's Word designed it.

chapter seven

transforming thoughts

The battlefield of the mind began in the garden with Eve and the serpent. Like a sneaky snake, the enemy disguised himself and slithered into her space, deceiving her mind and perception. He asked her a question and then gave her a half-true answer.

- **The question:** "Has God indeed said, 'You shall not eat of every tree of the garden'?" (Genesis 3:1).
- **The half-true answer:** "Then the serpent said to the woman, 'You will not surely die. For God knows that in the day you eat of it your eyes will be opened, and you will be like God, knowing good and evil'" (Genesis 3:4–5). Some of this was true. Yes, she would know good and evil. But what the deceiver left out was the pain, the brokenness, the weight of sin, and evil.

This is the same battle we fight with anxiety today. The enemy presents seemingly honest questions as we travel through this life. But then he offers up half-baked answers or no answers at all, leaving a platter of fear, anxiety, and desperation for us and our kids to wrestle with. He sends detours that seem safe, so we follow down his path leading us to question what we know.

Questions like:

- "Why can't I get it together?" The enemy's answer: You just need to focus more on yourself.
- "Why is everyone else's child capable of . . . ?" The enemy's answer: You need to give them what you never had as a child. Fill them with fun and freedom.
- "How do I get him/her to be calmer like that kid?" The enemy's answer: Your family is the only one. You must be failing as a parent. You should do better.

Answers like this one from the enemy are common. The devil is good at distorting what is true and seeks only to kill or destroy us through his deception (John 10:10). This often leads us to seek help desperately in any way we can find. If we only use the world's coping mechanisms or controlling thoughts, we are only able to change the mind part of the way. The truth is, we can probably nod at each other and know we've tried it all. Just the fact that you are this far into this book tells me you are doing exactly what you "should" as a parent. So take a deep breath and let's focus on the full truth. There is nothing worse than something that is baked halfway, which is the result we receive when the enemy answers our questions or we apply coping or controlling thoughts rather than God's truth to combat anxiety. The enemy leaves us with a gut punch of lies and we wallow in the fallout with a lack of faith and devastating frustration.

In *Rewire Your Anxious Brain*, the authors present the idea of "coping thoughts." If a person is to overcome anxiety, they must first identify an "anxiety-igniting thought" and then replace it with a "coping thought."[1] With this model in place, we can take the thought captive and replace it with something better. Rather than a coping thought, I want you to consider replacing the thought with a transformative thought.

Have you ever seen one of those little toy trucks that can be changed into a superhero just by a few moves? Nothing about the truck changes except the way the truck parts are moved. When each part of the truck is moved to the right place, the truck transforms into something different. It is literally called a transformer. This is a picture of what God can do in your child's mind. The child is still the same the child, but redirecting the thoughts to focus on God's truth transforms the child to have a different mentality and perspective on the current situation. When this happens, we see how God's Word gives us the full truth rather than half-truth. We find this picture in Romans 12:2 when Paul talks about a renewed mind: "And do not be conformed to this world, but be transformed by the renewing of your mind, that you may prove what is that good and acceptable and perfect will of God."

We can replace the anxious thought with God's truth. The power of God's Word doesn't just help us and our children *cope*. It transforms the mind.

We can replace the anxious thought with God's truth. The power of God's Word doesn't just help us and our children cope. It transforms the mind.

Let's take a look back at each of the questions again and answer them according to God's Word.

- "Why can't I get it together?"
  God's Word says, "I am the vine, you are the branches. He who abides in Me, and I in him, bears much fruit; for without Me you can do nothing" (John 15:5). We must look to Jesus for help. The answer is not in ourselves, but in Him.

  New thought: *I can "get it together" when I get together with Jesus.*

- "Why is everyone else's child capable of . . . ?"
  God's Word says, "For You formed my inward parts; You covered me in my mother's womb. I will praise You, for I am fearfully and wonderfully made; Marvelous are Your works, And that my soul knows very well" (Psalm 139:13–14). Your child has a unique set of God given strengths. In the weak areas, ask God for help.
  New thought: *My child has God-given strengths and is capable of . . .*

- "How do I get him/her to be calmer like their kid?"
  God's Word says, "The things which you learned and received and heard and saw in me, these do, and the God of peace will be with you" (Philippians 4:9). If you want your child to have more peace, ask the God of peace to show you how to lead your child to peace. As long as we stay tuned to the enemy and his lies, we will continue to struggle, unable to cope.

  New thought: *God is capable of helping my child.*

As you pray over your child's mind, pray that they would begin to believe God's truth about themselves and their fears. Sometimes it simply begins with us. In our sin nature, we often want control. If we do not fill our minds with God's Word, we will return to old thought patterns ourselves, sabotaging our own efforts of guiding our children. The hard work starts in our own hearts and minds as we pursue the peace of God for ourselves.

There is an active path toward peace found in Philippians 4:8 that teaches how to filter thoughts appropriately. This is a lifelong battle and not something you will arrive at one day never to return. It is a day-by-day, moment-by-moment journey for you and your child. It is not a "do better" kind of message.

The hard work starts in our own hearts and minds as we pursue the peace of God for ourselves.

Rather, it is a clear list of all the things to think about. It's kind of like when someone goes on a diet. Where most people fall off the bandwagon on any diet is by becoming consumed with what they cannot eat. If they could shift the mindset to focus on the good things they can have, they would be more satisfied and reach their dieting goals faster. The same principle applies for the mind.

Instead of a good food list, I have provided a good thought list from Philippians 4:8:

- Is it true?
- Is it noble?
- Is it just?
- Is it pure?
- Is it lovely?
- Is it a good report?
- Is it excellent?
- Is it worthy of praise?

These questions on the Good Thought list help us filter out the thoughts that sabotage our honest efforts of less anxiety and more peace. Life with an anxious child often seems like walking down a path with several options of detours ahead. There are multiple possibilities of landmines, but you never know when you might hit one. Detours can derail the child in a hot second if you aren't prepared or aware of what is going on. This explosive reality can leave us frustrated and tempted to start believing those old half-truths of the enemy. This is why transformative thought practice is so valuable.

Here is how we can practically make this work for our kids:

1. Name the anxious thought.

This might feel difficult for you and your child at first, but with practice, it will become second nature.

An example of what you can say: "I can see this is hard for you. Are you feeling angry, frustrated, afraid, or something else?"

Once the child names the emotion, it is time to evaluate the facts. Some children might need help putting words to their feelings.

2. Talk about the facts.

During this conversation, help lead your child toward the facts. Talk about what happened and where you are headed.

Say: "Let's talk about what happened." Then talk about the facts of the situation.

God gave us emotions and they are not bad—they just need to be evaluated and put through God's filter so we can respond respectfully and appropriately. Let's try it.

3. Put the emotions and facts through God's Good Thought filter.

You can use one or two from the Good Thought list to help lead your child to peace. Look back at the list and evaluate which one will work best for the situation. Often simply beginning with the first one on the list—*Is it true?*—is all you need to get your child to begin their transformative thought process. By focusing on what is true, the child can begin to look at life a little differently. But there is one more step to transformation that you and your child can do every time to get the mind to do the hard work of change. One thing that works wonders for our family is to remind each other to "tell yourself the truth."

4. Replace the anxious thought with God's truth.

This is where lasting transformation happens. Once the child has named the emotion tied to the anxious thought, talked about the facts, and put the facts through God's filter, God's truth is ready to stick to the situation.

Say: "Let's see what the Bible has to say about this."

To make this easy for you, I've included a God's Truth chart for you to use for your child's most common emotions in the Activities section following this chapter. If you don't see an emotion or thought on there that your child deals with, feel free to add it. When your child has a big emotion, you can help them learn to capture it and cast it down, leading them to obedience to Christ like we find in 2 Corinthians 10:5: "Casting down arguments and every high thing that exalts itself against the knowledge of God, bringing every thought into captivity to the obedience of Christ."

truth-telling time

Peace is not something we can manipulate or formulate. It is a gift God gives His children. Peace from God is promised to guard the heart and the mind. Max Lucado says it this way, "Our Father gives us the very peace of God. He downloads the tranquility of the throne room into our world, resulting in an inexplicable calm."[2]

> And the peace of God, which surpasses all understanding, will guard your hearts and minds through Christ Jesus. Finally, brethren, whatever things are true, whatever things are noble, whatever things are just, whatever things are pure, whatever things are lovely, whatever things are of good report, if there is any virtue and if there is anything praiseworthy—meditate on these things. The things which you learned and received and heard and saw in me, these do, and the God of peace will be with you. (Philippians 4:7–9)

> Peace is not something we can manipulate or formulate. It is a gift God gives His children.

We cannot lock down our own hearts and minds, and neither can our children. That is God's job to do with God's peace. We need God's truth to impact our lives in a personal way so we can experience His peace. One of the first steps is to name the anxious thought for what it is and replace it with God's truth. This is when all of us can begin to experience transformational peace, when we remind ourselves what is true. God's Word has the power to transform minds, even your anxious child's.

☆ all-star tip

Have your child write down or draw something that makes them feel anxious. Help them if they can't think of something specific. Identify God's truth to combat the anxious thought. Before they let anxious thoughts consume them next time, choose one of God's truths that is most applicable to your child's needs. Print it out or write it out and put it somewhere visible in your home. Use it regularly multiple times a day until they begin to use it themselves. Have your child write it out and make a colorful picture of it, or you write it out and have your child decorate the page with stickers. Do what works for your family to make it memorable and usable.

One that is used regularly in our home in response to common fears is Psalm 56:3, "Whenever I am afraid, I will trust in You." We use this at bedtime, for school anxiety, social anxiety, or anytime fear is the focus.

Finding the feeling and replacing it with God's truth will work wonders to take your child from tense to transformed.

a ray of sunshine

Lord, Help me today. I know the devil wants me to think that You don't love me or really care about me. But Your Word says, "For God so loved the world that He gave His only begotten Son that whosoever believeth in Him should not perish but have everlasting life." In Jesus' name, amen.

parent heart check

What is one of God's truths you need as a parent in this season? Choose a verse and write it in your journal. Use the Emotion Chart in the Activities section if needed.

Answer these questions in your journal:

- How can you remind yourself of this truth daily?
- What is one of God's truths your child needs most right now?
- How can you and your child work toward reminding each other of the truth?

Write or say a prayer only saying what is true about God. No questions. Only statements about who God is and what He can do.

game plan highlights

- God's Word has the power to transform minds.
- We can replace the anxious thought with God's truth. The power of God's Word doesn't just help us and our children cope. It transforms the mind.
- We must look to Jesus for help. The answer is not in ourselves, but in Him.
- Your child has a unique set of God given strengths. In the weak areas, ask God for help.
- If you want your child to have more peace, ask the God of peace to show you how to lead your child to peace.
- Finding the feeling and replacing it with God's truth will work wonders to take your child from tense to transformed.

Weekly Prayer Guide for My Child's Mind

Instructions: Use the prayer guide below by praying the prayers provided or create your own.

Sunday: True Thoughts

God, please help my child believe what is true. Help me as I present the truth of Your Word to them. Open their minds to the way You can help them. When I am not with them, give them wisdom to discern what is true. In Jesus' name, amen.

Monday: Pure Thoughts

God, please help my child focus their thoughts on things that are pure. Guard their minds from ungodliness and sin. When impurity is presented to them, help them turn away and turn to You. In Jesus' name, amen.

Tuesday: Lovely Thoughts

God, please help my child think on things that are lovely. In a world where hate is present and wickedness is all around them, give them tangible experiences that help them see and experience godly love in action. In Jesus' name, amen.

Wednesday: Good Report Thoughts

God, please help my child to focus on good things. Rumors, lies, and unkindness will always be accessible. Help them be the one who stands up for good. When they have the choice, give them strength to make the right choice. In Jesus' name, amen.

Thursday: Excellent Thoughts

God, please help my child's thoughts to be excellent. I know they are capable of so much. Please help them use their knowledge and wisdom in a way that honors You. In Jesus' name, amen.

Friday: Praiseworthy Thoughts

God, please help my child to praise You. When everyone around them is complaining or being disagreeable, help them see the good in You. Help them lift You high even when no one around them understands. In Jesus' name, amen.

Saturday: Gratitude Thoughts

God, please help my child practice gratitude. Help them see Your blessings in their life. Give them a heart, mind, and mouth that overflows with thanksgiving. In Jesus' name, amen.

Activities for Parents & Children

Since this section is about the mind, the activities are less about actively doing something and more about the hard work of how to think. These will take intentional conversations and time. Make the time to work through these regularly and it will pay off.

Activity 5: Practicing What-Is Statements

Instructions: Together with your child, come up with three what-if questions that are used in your family regularly.

- What if I lose?
- What if I can't do it?
- What if they don't like me?

Work together to replace those what-if questions with what-is statements.

For example:

- My team is doing their best. I am doing my best. That is what matters most.
- My mind is strong and I can try. Even if it is difficult, I can practice and get better.
- Unkindness is usually not about me but about something going on with them.

Now create your own by filling in what-if and what-is questions and statements with your child.

What if . . .

1.

2.

3.

What is . . .

1.

2.

3.

Activity 6: Practicing Gratitude

Instructions for Gratitude Activity 1: Use the space below to help your child make a Gratitude List. Write or draw ten things you are thankful for.

1. ____________________

2. ____________________

3. ____________________

4. ____________________

5. ____________________

6. ____________________

7. ____________________

8. ____________________

9. ____________________

10. ____________________

Instructions for Gratitude Activity 2: Purchase or create cards of gratitude. Think of three people you and your child can write notes of gratitude to. Consider these things when coming up with the people:

- Who has spoken a kind or encouraging word?
- Who has noticed you or who have you noticed doing something good?
- Who did something kind for you?
- Who serves at your school, church, or in your community?
- Who needs a word of appreciation?

Write down the names of the three people here:

1. ______________________________

2. ______________________________

3. ______________________________

If your child needs help, have them use this template to write the gratitude note or create their own.

Dear [insert name],

I want to thank you for [insert what you want to thank them for]. Your kindness has impacted me because [explain why you are thankful for what they did or do]. I appreciate you and want you to know how thankful I am for you. [Complete the note with your own words.]

Sincerely,
[Insert your name]
Choose a date when you will deliver the note or put it in the mailbox.

Activity 7: Practicing Good Thoughts

Instructions for Practicing Good Thoughts Activity 1: Read the poem to your child and talk about a specific time you can pray with your child. Stop right now and pray with them or ask them if they would like to pray and thank God for helping with their thoughts.

Good Thoughts Poem

I have thoughts every day
Some are good
Some are gray

Some go fast
Some like to stay

No matter what
Good thoughts or bad

I can trust God
I don't have to be sad

I can believe
I can know

God is with me to stay
When I feel afraid
I can pray

Instructions for Practicing Good Thoughts Activity 2:

Step 1: Use the chart provided below to identify two big feelings you or your child experienced this week.

Step 2: Use the verses provided in the chart to combat that thought daily this week. If your child is able to, have them write it down or type it out and print it. Let your child color or paint or design it. Put it somewhere visible in the house where you both will see it. Review it daily.

Step 3: Together, create a one-sentence truth statement about what they can do and about what God can do that summarizes the truth of the verse. Keep it simple and short and use each one regularly. Use the ones provided in the chart for quick reference.

Angry

"Take My yoke upon you and learn from Me, for I am gentle and lowly in heart, and you will find rest for your souls." (Matthew 11:29)
Truth statement about God: God is gentle.
"A soft answer turns away wrath, but a harsh word stirs up anger." (Proverbs 15:1)
Truth statement about me: I can respond calmly.

Afraid

"Fear not, for I am with you; Be not dismayed, for I am your God. I will strengthen you, Yes, I will help you, I will uphold you with My righteous right hand." (Isaiah 41:10)

Truth statement about God: God is with me and will help me.
"Whenever I am afraid, I will trust in You." (Psalm 56:3)
Truth statement about me: I can trust God.

Anxious

"O Lord, You have searched me and known me. You know my sitting down and my rising up; You understand my thought afar off." (Psalm 139:1–2)
Truth statement about God: God already knows everything that will happen.
"Do not be anxious about anything, but in everything by prayer and supplication with thanksgiving let your requests be made known to God." (Philippians 4:6 ESV)
Truth statement about me: I can be thankful and pray because God already knows.

Ashamed

"For God did not send His Son into the world to condemn the world, but that the world through Him might be saved." (John 3:17)
Truth statement about God: God loves me and wants to forgive me.
"If we confess our sins, He is faithful and just to forgive us our sins and to cleanse us from all unrighteousness." (1 John 1:9)
Truth statement about me: I can confess my sin. God will forgive me.

Bitter

"The Lord is merciful and gracious, slow to anger, and abounding in mercy." (Psalm 103:8)
Truth statement about God: God is merciful.
"Let all bitterness and wrath and anger and clamor and slander be put away from you, along with all malice. Be kind to one another, tenderhearted, forgiving one another, as God in Christ forgave you." (Ephesians 4:31–32 ESV)
Truth statement about me: I can let it go. I can be merciful.

Conflicted

"You will keep him in perfect peace, Whose mind is stayed on You, Because he trusts in You." (Isaiah 26:3)
Truth statement about God: God gives peace.
"If possible, so far as it depends on you, live peaceably with all." (Romans 12:18 ESV)
Truth statement about me: I can get along.

Confused

"For God is not a God of confusion but of peace. As in all the churches of the saints." (1 Corinthians 14:33 ESV)
Truth statement about God: God is not surprised or perplexed.
"So then faith comes by hearing, and hearing by the word of God." (Romans 10:17)
Truth statement about me: I can believe God's Word gives me clarity and truth.

Discouraged

"Be of good courage, and He shall strengthen your heart, all you who hope in the Lord." (Psalm 31:24)

Truth statement about God: God is my strength.

"Have I not commanded you? Be strong and of good courage; do not be afraid, nor be dismayed, for the Lord your God is with you wherever you go." (Joshua 1:9)

Truth statement about me: I can have courage.

Doubting

"As for God, His way is perfect; the word of the Lord is proven; He is a shield to all who trust in Him." (Psalm 18:30)

Truth statement about God: God's Word is trustworthy.

"If any of you lacks wisdom, let him ask God, who gives generously to all without reproach, and it will be given him. But let him ask in faith, with no doubting, for the one who doubts is like a wave of the sea that is driven and tossed by the wind." (James 1:5–6 ESV)

Truth statement about me: I will ask God. He gives wisdom.

Hopeless

"For You are my hope, O Lord God; You are my trust from my youth." (Psalm 71:5)

Truth statement about God: God gives me hope.

"May the God of hope fill you with all joy and peace in believing, so that by the power of the Holy Spirit you may abound in hope." (Romans 15:13 ESV)

Truth statement about me: I believe God gives me hope.

Impatient

"He has made everything beautiful in its time. Also He has put eternity in their hearts, except that no one can find out the work that God does from beginning to end." (Ecclesiastes 3:11)

Truth statement about God: God's timing is always perfect.

"Be still before the Lord and wait patiently for him; fret not yourself over the one who prospers in his way, over the man who carries out evil devices!" (Psalm 37:7 ESV)

Truth statement about me: I will be still and wait for God's perfect timing.

Lonely

"Let your conduct be without covetousness; be content with such things as you have. For He Himself has said, 'I will never leave you nor forsake you.'" (Hebrews 13:5)

Truth statement about God: God will never leave me.

"No man shall be able to stand before you all the days of your life. Just as I was with Moses, so I will be with you. I will not leave you or forsake you." (Joshua 1:5 ESV)

Truth statement about me: I believe God is with me.

Mistreated

"He was oppressed and He was afflicted, yet He opened not His mouth; He was led as a lamb to the slaughter, and as a sheep before its shearers is silent, so He opened not His mouth."
(Isaiah 53:7)

Truth statement about God: God understands what I am going through.

"But I say to you, Love your enemies and pray for those who persecute you." (Matthew 5:44 ESV)
Truth statement about me: I can love and pray for people that are not kind.

Misunderstood

"As for you, my son Solomon, know the God of your father, and serve Him with a loyal heart and with a willing mind; for the LORD searches all hearts and understands all the intent of the thoughts. If you seek Him, He will be found by you; but if you forsake Him, He will cast you off forever." (1 Chronicles 28:9)
Truth statement about God: God always understands and sees the heart of people.
"But you, O LORD, know me; you see me, and test my heart toward you." (Jeremiah 12:3 ESV)
Truth statement about me: I believe God understands me even when others don't.

Needy

"For He will deliver the needy when he cries, the poor also, and him who has no helper." (Psalm 72:12)
Truth statement about God: God is the deliverer.
"Fear not, for I am with you; be not dismayed, for I am your God; I will strengthen you, yes, I will help you, I will uphold you with my righteous right hand." (Isaiah 41:10)
Truth statement about me: I need God's help.

Resentful

"The Lord is not slow to fulfill his promise as some count slowness, but is patient toward you, not wishing that any should perish, but that all should reach repentance." (2 Peter 3:9 ESV)

Truth statement about God: God is patient and wants the best for everyone.

"See to it that no one fails to obtain the grace of God; that no 'root of bitterness' springs up and causes trouble, and by it many become defiled." (Hebrews 12:15 ESV)

Truth statement about me: I can be patient with other people and not hold grudges.

Sick

"Heal me, O LORD, and I shall be healed; save me, and I shall be saved, for You are my praise." (Jeremiah 17:14)

Truth statement about God: God is the healer.

"The LORD sustains him on his sickbed; in his illness you restore him to full health." (Psalm 41:3 ESV)

Truth statement about me: I believe God is in control.

Sinful

"But God demonstrates His own love toward us, in that while we were still sinners, Christ died for us." (Romans 5:8)

Truth statement about God: God sent Jesus for sinners.

"Create in me a clean heart, O God, and renew a right spirit within me." (Psalm 51:10 ESV)

Truth statement about me: I believe God will forgive my sin.

Stupid

"For the LORD gives wisdom; from His mouth come knowledge and understanding." (Proverbs 2:6)

Truth statement about God: God has all the answers.

"The fear of the LORD is the beginning of knowledge; but fools despise wisdom and instruction." (Proverbs 1:7)

Truth statement about me: I believe God gives me wisdom and understanding.

Tired

"He makes me to lie down in green pastures; He leads me beside the still waters." (Psalm 23:2)

Truth statement about God: God leads to rest.

"Come to me, all who labor and are heavy laden, and I will give you rest." (Matthew 11:28 ESV)

Truth statement about me: I believe God gives me rest.

Unloved

"He who does not love does not know God, for God is love." (1 John 4:8)

Truth statement about God: God is love.

"For I am sure that neither death nor life, nor angels nor rulers, nor things present nor things to come, nor powers, nor height nor depth, nor anything else in all creation, will be able to separate us from the love of God in Christ Jesus our Lord." (Romans 8:38–39 ESV)

Truth statement about me: I believe God loves me.

Upset

"I called on the Lord in distress; The Lord answered me and set me in a broad place." (Psalm 118:5)

Truth statement about God: God hears the cries of His children.

"The Lord is near to the brokenhearted and saves the crushed in spirit." (Psalm 34:18 ESV)

Truth statement about me: I believe God is close to me and hears me.

part three

game plan for calming the soul

chapter eight

the soul's source of calm

I wanted my love to be enough for my child. I did what any good mom would do, offering comfort and help. I stayed within arm's reach. Hovering closely every time my child struggled. I wanted my child to know that when no one else understood, I was there. And I would *always* be there.

When chaos continued and my child still struggled with debilitating anxiety, I thought maybe I just wasn't cut out for this. Maybe this was just too hard.

These intrusive thoughts and lies from the enemy creep into parents' minds especially when our kid seems to be the only one who is having a hard time. When an activity is supposed to be fun, but fun always turns into fears, life feels complicated. It is frustrating to look forward to something only for it to turn into tears and anger.

It compels parents to struggle with confidence and curates a culture of anything but calm.

I eventually came to a point where I began to release my grip. You know the grip. It's tight. It is as if the outcome of this child's entire life depends on you. For me, it was letting him go play with other kids without being within earshot of every word said. If I could sit with you right now, I would reach my hand over to yours and have you look square into my eyes. I want to give you a sentence of advice I once heard that stuck with me like a permanent tattoo. I don't have any tattoos, but if I got one it might say what I am about to tell you. Open your heart and hear these words with all the sincerity in the world that I mean them: You are not the Savior. You cannot rescue your child from every fear. You cannot save them. You cannot manipulate or transform your child with your willpower and determination. With all the fiery passion and perseverance of a determined mama bear, saving is still only up to the Savior. Not you and not me.

> You are not the Savior. . . . Only God can make your child into the amazing person He created them to be.

There is only one Savior. His name is Jesus. We can lead and guide. Give choices. Take our kids to therapy. Train. Practice. Stop, breathe, and think. Give medication. Work through meltdowns. . . . But we cannot save.

There comes a point when we have to start surrendering our own abilities of everything depending on us. It is the surrender of saving. Sometimes we don't even realize we are carrying the weight of a rescuer. We think maybe something we do or don't do is going to mess them up, or make them all they were meant to be. But only God can make them into the amazing person He created them to be. With or without a mom or dad, God has the power to reach down into your child's heart and speak directly to them, shaping them into His masterpiece.

Take the pressure off yourself. This does not mean we stop parenting and discipling or give up the tips and tricks we've learned along the way. It means the opposite. God has placed you in their life to parent them. It means we let go of the idea that if we mess up, they will be messed up. It means we lay down the idea that this burden is too heavy to carry and we let God do the heavy lifting. It means we stop priding ourselves as if we are our child's saving grace. We let go of the social, educational, emotional, and spiritual pressure we have often placed on ourselves and look to God for every answer we need. We place the child in God's hands, where they have belonged all along. We trust that in time, God will help.

We have to change our perspective and our thinking about calming our children. Parenting, especially parenting an anxious child, is less about doing everything right. It is more about realizing the child has the ability to learn to regulate their own emotions. Aside from us and alongside their Creator, they can do this.

It has a lot to do with letting go. There is probably some very specific *letting go* that needs to happen in your parenting. I only know this because I have experienced it. I have held on so tightly that in some seasons I believed my child could not go anywhere or be left with anyone without me. I don't mean you step back and don't do anything. But I do mean you step back in some of the anxious moments and let your child work through it for themselves. You've given them the tools. It might be time to let them attempt to use them. You've prayed the prayers.

> "I, even I, am the Lord, and besides Me there is no savior." (Isaiah 43:11)

Jesus the Savior is the One true source of calm our children need. God is a much better transformer from chaos to calm than you or me. If we try to take on the responsibility of saving, we will be frustrated or irritated and our children will be too.

Practically speaking this might look a little different for each of us depending on your child's needs and abilities. For all of us it looks like making changes on the outside and the inside.

Here is how applying this might make more sense. Take each of these steps at your own pace.

How to Embrace the Soul's Source of Calm—Jesus

1. Surrender the moment. Surrender every anxious episode, thought, or struggle to God's control. Give your child and every behavior, reaction, and moment to God. Choose to look to Jesus over looking at how you can swoop in and rescue, fix, or formulate a result. It is an internal decision that will show on the outside. It takes root when we act on the surrender externally. It requires letting go of the moment to let your child decide if they will use the coping tools they have or if they will give into their big feelings.

Sometimes it is the little things like putting on their own socks or the big things like filling out their own job application. These skills might seem basic, but for a child with anxiety the fear of how the sock might not be perfectly straight if Mom doesn't do it just right can feel really big. For the job application, there is the fear that if they mess it up they won't get the job. When we let them do it themselves, a couple things happen. They realize they can. They learn how to do things the right way eventually. Mistakes have a way of being our best teachers. They will be more apt to try next time when they realize they can do it themselves.

The anxious thoughts of *what if I can't* or *what if I fail* will keep them bound until we surrender the moment and let them try. If they can possibly do it without help, let them. Release the desire to have them do things perfectly or without a struggle. Let them struggle. Let them do hard things. It won't hurt them. It will help them gain confidence and reliance on God's strength. As long as you remain a crutch every time they need something, they can never learn what God can do through and with them.

> As long as you remain a crutch every time they need something, they can never learn what God can do through and with them.

2. Let go. Let go of the weight of your child's anxiety. We have all carried it much longer than necessary. It means letting go of making excuses as to why your child is the way they are. There might be real reasons, diagnosis, trauma, or history. We cannot let these things dominate life to the point that we give in to the belief that there is no hope. Let go of making provision for the meltdowns. Let go of avoiding hard things because they are just too hard. Let go of carrying every moment in your arms and on your chest as a burden you were somehow called to bear as the parent of an anxious child. Let go of the mentality that this is just the way things are. Let go of what other people think about you and how you parent your child. Release other people's expectations of you and your child.

This letting go is radical and spiritual. It is fully believing we are not the Savior but God is. It is choosing on the inside to step back. To let go. To release our child and their future to God without restraint. Complete surrender says, "I can't save, but God can."

3. Rely on God's help. Tell God about it. Say, *God, this is your child. You know them better than I do. You know what they need at this moment. Help them see beyond the current anxiety all the way to You.*

While their salvation isn't up to you, your prayers hold the power to move the heart of God.

Understanding you cannot change your child's feelings, thoughts, or actions, but God can, will take you to a new place in your parenting. **God can do what you can't.** He is present when you can't be. He sees it all. Let me say it one more time just in case you are struggling to believe it—you are not the Savior.

Jesus is able to do more for your child than you could ever imagine. When I hear Ray pray for his own struggles, I see God doing something I cannot do. I feel God moving in his life and his heart. If you only take one thing from this book because it all just feels too hard. Take this—**God is able to help your child, so ask Him to.** *God, please help my child* is one of the most powerful things you can pray for the child you deeply love. Pray for them like their life depends on it. Because while their salvation isn't up to you, your prayers hold the power to move the heart of God.

truth-telling time

Confess your trespasses to one another, and pray for one another, that you may be healed. The effective, fervent prayer of a righteous man avails much.

(JAMES 5:16)

If you've felt like everything depends on you, take time to confess it to God and a close friend or family member. And then pray your heart out. Beg God for direction, answers, help, and healing. God's answers don't always fall in our laps through perfectly wrapped gifts, checks in the mail, or clouds aligned in the sky, but sometimes they come through our children's little moments of victory. It's when you see them walk into a room with confidence for the first time. Or when they hold it together in the face of a fear they often melted down over. It's when they come close and are able to tell you how they feel. It's when they bow their heads and ask God for themselves for help. It's when they say, "Mom, we should pray right now."

I know these little victories because I've experienced them with my children. We still have struggles, and life is far from perfect. But God's work in our home and family is undeniable. And I fully believe and have faith God can help your child too. Don't give up too soon. Pray again and again and again.

☆ all-star tip

Next time you want to swoop in and rescue your child from a difficult moment, pause. Take a deep breath. Practice your own stop, breathe, and think moment. And pray instead. You might still need to step in to correct or guide, but don't do it without praying first.

a ray of sunshine

Dear God, thank You for my life. You created the whole world, and I am so blessed that I have You in my life. Thank You for sending Your own Son to die on the cross to save us from our sins. And Lord, thank You for giving us a choice to follow You. Help those who don't know You to know You. In Jesus' name, amen.

parent heart check

Think of ways you have considered yourself the only hope for your child. Write them down in your journal.

Thoughtfully answer the following questions in your journal:

- Who is the Savior of you and your child?
- How does letting go of the Savior mentality help you think differently about the way you will parent your child?
- How does it help you to let go of the Savior mentality?
- Is this change hard for you? What makes it most difficult?

Take time this week to look for the little victories. Write them down and go back to them when you start feeling the pressure that all depends on you. Because it will come back. But when it does, tell yourself the truth—you are not the Savior.

game plan highlights

- You are not the Savior.
- Only God can make them into the amazing person He created them to be.
- Take the pressure off yourself.
- Jesus the Savior is the One true source of calm our children need.
- God is able to help your child, so ask Him to.

chapter nine

the soul's process of calm

I tucked my young child into bed. We said our prayers and sang our songs. He drifted off to a peaceful sleep. I settled into my own rest for the night. And then it happened. I bolted out of bed to the sound of my child screaming in terror. Stepping on a Lego in the hallway, knocking my head on the doorframe of his bedroom, and tripping over clothing left out the night before, I landed right beside his bed, head throbbing and foot fresh with pain.

Nightmares and night terrors are truly terrible. It's hard to understand and doctors can't really explain why they happen at certain seasons during childhood. They can be brought on by various stressors, but there is rarely a cure to help these nighttime episodes settle down. They tend to happen most in children ages one through twelve years old.[1] My child's nighttime terror was hard to soothe, difficult to predict, and complicated to deal with, especially with Legos and Matchbox cars along the way.

I sat beside his bed soothing my banged-up forehead and foot as his little hand reached out for me. I grabbed his hand in mine, and he quickly draped both arms around my neck. I pulled him close and wiped the sweat from his forehead and tears from his eyes. We rocked back and forth until his crying calmed. Searching for the words to say, I whispered to him, "Did you have a bad dream?" He answered through his still tear-filled breaths, "There was a lion. And a bear."

"Was there anyone else?"

He lifted his head and looked straight into my eyes. With fear still all over him, he said, "Jesus was here. He told them to leave."

I call moments like these sacred moments. These are the moments when spiritual warfare is happening in real time, and we have an open door to teach our children how to fight their fears with God's help. These moments of shepherding little hearts gives parents an amazing opportunity to speak truth and power over a child's anxieties and unknowns.

While daytime struggles can consume our efforts and lead to exhaustion, the nighttime battles have a potential to give us a deeper understanding of what they are facing. There is a very real spiritual battle going on.

> For we do not wrestle against flesh and blood, but against principalities, against powers, against the rulers of the darkness of this age, against spiritual hosts of wickedness in the heavenly places. (Ephesians 6:12)

This is a fight they need your help and guidance through. For our family, this meant letting my son know He could ask Jesus for help. Not just for help to cope better during the day but help for his nighttime battles that terrorized him.

There are constant current events that cause daytime and nighttime stressors. While we can try to protect our children from obvious triggers, we cannot always avoid them. There is value and potential for growth when we help our children face their triggers.

When we go to God with our child amidst anxious moments, we are modeling how to fight anxiety biblically.

This means we talk about it. We do not tuck it away. We do not pretend it did not happen. We do not sweep it under the rug. It means I, as Mom, lead my child into the battle and choose to bring up the bear and the lion again. But not as a means for triggering more night terror, but as a means for telling my child the truth about Jesus. Jesus was there that night to protect and to defend. His presence was purposeful and powerful. This moment for our family became a lifeline of help for the nighttime madness that had gone on too long. This was a "God is with you" teaching moment. When our children embrace for themselves that God is with them, they have a powerful arsenal of hope in their tool kit to combat anxiety.

Our bedtime prayers changed from "Help us sleep well" to "In the mighty name of Jesus, we ask for every evil spirit to leave this house right now." You as the parent have a very big responsibility to look beyond the surface level fears and see the battle going on in the darkness of your child's soul. If your child speaks of spiritual things, pretend creatures, or heavenly beings, lean in and listen closely. Do not dismiss it. Be attentive to the language and the verbiage they use. Acknowledge what they say and experience and get ready to fight the spiritual battle with them. When we go to God with our child amidst anxious moments, we are modeling how to fight anxiety biblically.

Each of my children has said things about God, the devil, heaven, and spiritual battles at very young ages. To be a Christian parent means we will engage in spiritual battles that have eternal ramifications. This should not ignite fear in your heart, but it should light a fire in your soul to fight on your knees like a warrior who holds the keys to the war. Your prayers can change things.

Rather than always praying, "God, please don't let my child have any nightmares," change the narrative of the prayers toward what God can do in your child *if the nightmares persist.* Do not let your prayers be words of worry. Rather turn them into words of worship and holy warfare. Guide your child from coping strategies to Christ. It is about teaching our children not to avoid the stressors or triggers in their life, but to abide with Christ in them. To lead a child to face their fears with faith in God alone changes the pressure for us and our children. For us, it is no longer about being a perfect parent. It is about pointing the child to a perfect God. For them it is no longer about doing what they need to cope. It is about getting closer to Christ.

Avoidance is a very real coping technique that many people naturally turn to. If we avoid stressors, we think it means we will experience less stress. But this inhibits our children by only giving them limited experiences to truly deal with real life. When we face anxiety this way repeatedly, we teach children that they can't handle certain situations. A better way is to teach them that with Christ they can do anything. We want our children to learn full dependence on and victory in Christ. But sometimes we have to learn it for ourselves first. By avoiding anxiety or situations that make us feel anxious, we are only maintaining anxiety.[2]

Guide your child from coping strategies to Christ.

Pastor Charles Stanley gives it to us this way, "Worrying focuses our attention on our circumstances; God wants our attention focused on Him. In fact, He never wants us to focus on the person or thing for which He has burdened us."[3]

Practically applying this is simple yet challenging. The reason is because it makes us flip the script of what we naturally do. We tend to focus solely on our child, their behaviors, external triggers, or controlling the moment and environment.

When it comes to spiritual battles, we do not have control. God does. While this should bring us great comfort, it requires releasing the tight grip of unknown possibilities. It goes all the way back to the what-ifs we talked about in the beginning of this book. Rather than settle into a thought process of my child has terrors, or trauma, or is troubled, let's speak the truth over them.

Here is what this might look like:

- **Ask your child direct questions.**
  For example, ask, "Did you have a bad dream?"
  But do not stop here. Follow up by asking about the details. While not every nightmare will be like my child's with Jesus fighting the battle, every dream explained gives you and your child a deeper connection.[4] It is a way for you to connect and give them a voice to what is going on inside them.

- **Talk about the anxiety they are feeling.**
  For example, ask, "How did the dream make you feel?"
  Talk about how it is normal to have feelings that are strong, especially during or after a bad dream.
  "Does it make you feel safe or unsure?"
  Remind your child it is normal to feel unsure or afraid. But we have a choice how we respond to those feelings.
  Use a personal story to connect. For example, "I have had a bad dream before too . . ." Explain how bad dreams do not control us or reflect who we are.
- **Tell the truth.**
  For example, say, "Mom (or Dad) is here with you. You know who else is here? God is. Even when your parents can't be right here, you can ask God for help."

Truth is the key to help your child find hope. They want to know that they will be okay. That they are safe. That you understand and are for them. Tell them God is for them. He can help them.

Teach them words of the wise Solomon in Proverbs 3:24, "When you lie down, you will not be afraid; yes, you will lie down and your sleep will be sweet." Say it and pray it over your child.

Praying and speaking truth over your child does not mean they will never have another bad dream, but it does mean they can use God's Word as a weapon in their battle.

truth-telling time

In Matthew 4, we find the story of Jesus being tempted by the devil in the wilderness. This was both a physical and spiritual battle. Physical because Jesus had not eaten for forty days. Spiritual because it was God's power versus the devil's. In each temptation that the enemy threw at Jesus, Jesus had a similar response. Every time He spoke directly to the enemy, He used the Word of God as His weapon.

> For the word of God is living and powerful, and sharper than any two-edged sword, piercing even to the division of soul and spirit, and of joints and marrow, and is a discerner of the thoughts and intents of the heart. (Hebrews 4:12)

This is the power we and our children can hold. God's Word is something you most likely have in your home. If not, get a copy today. Open it and find out what God has to say about the battle. All through God's Word, we find warfare. Your child's anxiety, while it could be chemically induced, is often not a battle of the flesh. While sometimes it might require medication, what we are discussing is the spiritual aspect of the struggle. Get the medication your child needs, but do not avoid the spiritual aspect of your child's mental health. This battle is an invisible war. Our children's greatest weapon for the battles they face is God's Word. Here are a few places in Scripture you can take your child for quick reference. Choose one to commit to memory with your child to equip them for everyday use:

Our children's greatest weapon for the battles they face is God's Word.

> Fear not, for I am with you;
> Be not dismayed, for I am your God.
> I will strengthen you,
> Yes, I will help you,

I will uphold you with My righteous right hand. (Isaiah 41:10)

I will lift up my eyes to the hills—
From whence comes my help?
My help comes from the Lord,
Who made heaven and earth. (Psalm 121:1–2)

God is our refuge and strength,
A very present help in trouble. (Psalm 46:1)

No one can overdose on God's Word. Nor can we ever overdose on communication with God. So get on your knees. Beg God. Let your child hear the cry of your heart. Show them what it looks like to go to battle for their emotions, their mind, their body, their soul. Christ is the cure for you and for me. And Christ is enough for your child.

Give them Jesus. Morning. Noon. Night. Snacktime. Bedtime. Playtime. All the time.

☆ all-star tip

Create a daily habit of including Jesus in your conversations. Pray for mealtime and bedtime. But don't stop there. When anything threatens you or your child, stop in the moment and take it to God in prayer. Use the weekly prayer calendars in the back of each section to get the conversation started daily.

a ray of sunshine

Lord, I have been through some rough times, but You brought me out of those rough times. Your mercy never fails me. Thank You for everything, Lord. All my days I will follow You. No turning back. In Jesus' name, amen.

parent heart check

Take out your journal and consider these questions:

- When is the last time you had a conversation about Jesus with your child?
- How can you implement Jesus conversations into your everyday routine?
- Do you find it difficult to talk about spiritual things? Why or why not?

game plan highlights

- Your prayers can change things.
- Guide your child from coping strategies to Christ.
- We want our children to learn full dependence on and victory in Christ. But sometimes we have to learn it for ourselves first.
- We cannot overdose on God's Word.

chapter ten

the soul's control of calm

"You are in charge."

These are the words that rolled out of my mouth to my child in the heated moment of a major meltdown. Her eyes darted back at mine in shock. Her screaming abruptly went quiet. Her body froze. My gaze held steady as I repeated the words again. "You are in charge."

I never thought this would be one of my parenting tips. Sometimes we as the parents need to remember we are the parent and we are in charge, but in this moment, I flipped the script. I call this teaching *soul control.* There are so many things we can teach our children, but soul control might be one of the most important skills they learn and embrace.

Soul control is different from self-control or emotional management. It is a way of owning their reactions. Soul control is choosing to embrace the consequences of their emotional expressions. Soul control is not a battle of the wills. It is teaching the child they have control over their body, mind, words, and spirit. They can surrender to God, obtaining self-control through the Spirit of God or keep fighting and acting out in the flesh. They have the choice.

> Soul control is choosing to embrace the consequences of their emotional expressions.

Helping our kids stay out of dangerous situations due to a lack of soul control begins by teaching soul control through the power of God in their lives. It is more than just about controlling the body. It goes deeper than controlling a back talker or a defiant preteen. Soul control is teaching children they have full responsibility for how they behave with their brains and bodies. And God can help them. With soul control, they have to face the consequences of what they think, do, and say.

When a child can begin to have agency, and feel some level of control over their actions, reactions, body, mind, and soul, this helps them make different choices. When they realize God gives them power like David over Goliath when it comes to their fears, they gain a fresh confidence to respond under control by God's power. There are things that anxiety offers that make a person feel out of control. It's the panic attacks that grip the throat or rush of fear over the entire body that makes it freeze or fight. But there is a better way to help our children face their giants.

Once a child has learned basic coping strategies and has a spiritual realization that God can help, it is time to expect them to begin tapping into the power God offers them. Parents can help a child learn this by modeling it, teaching it, and practicing it with the child repeatedly. One of the first steps toward soul control is teaching the child, "You are in charge and will have to deal with the consequences of your words and actions."

Here is a more specific breakdown of what they are in charge of:

- **Their Body**

  This means there is no hitting, kicking, biting, pinching, throwing ourselves on the floor, or acting out of control, because you are in charge of your body. You tell it what to do. If you feel like hitting, you get to tell yourself the truth that hitting will hurt others and have a negative consequence. A better option might be hitting a pillow or punching bag. At the end of long day of parenting, sometimes I feel like throwing myself on the floor and having a good fit or pity party.

This practice of soul control, like most tips in this book, isn't only for the kids. You are in charge of your actions too and you are your child's primary example on how to have soul control. Professionals agree that appropriate emotional response can be taught and improved when a parent practices regulating their emotions first.[1]

- **Their Mind**

  This one is more difficult for some because you cannot read your child's mind. But you can teach healthy thinking patterns. One way to fight negative thought patterns is to practice the principles we talked about in Part 2. As a way of review, it means we choose gratitude regularly. You too, Mom and Dad. Choose gratitude today over the thoughts that tell you that you aren't doing enough. Capture the bad thought and replace it with God's truth. You get to be the boss.

My youngest little one struggles with certain thought patterns that come back night after night. One of the things that helps her is to nightly remind her to "stay and pray." What this means is "stay in your bed and pray about what is bothering you." It takes her mind off the scary thought and places her mind on Jesus instead.

We find this truth in God's Word in Isaiah 26:3,"You will keep him in perfect peace, whose mind is stayed on you, Because he trusts in You." Staying and praying is changing a negative pattern of fear to faith. While she still wrestles with anxious thoughts, this is a pattern we are practicing to help reframe her fears. We as parents hold a great responsibility to continue to provide tools even if the battles keep coming. It's up to God to implement lasting change.

- **Their Words**

  I stood in the psych ward of the hospital and heard the words being slung by the man who was out of his mind. My ears were shocked by the sound of his voice and vile words coming out of his mouth. His body matched the words he spewed out like knives through the corridor. It took four strong grown men to pin him down. This is a prime example of a man who was clearly out of control in every way. We want to teach our children that with God's help they can absolutely be in control of the body, the mind, the words, and the soul that God has given them.

They do not have to let anxiety win. They do not have to surrender to tantrums, physical violence, self-harm, or intense anger.

They can surrender all the enormous feelings to Jesus. When we surrender to Jesus, our words sound different. He changes everything. I used to say things like, "My child would never . . ." or "If I were their mom, I would . . ." I've found God has changed me more by learning to care for and love my children through their battles than any other experience in my life. And I have a feeling He is changing you too.

My words about how others parent their kids sound different now. Our children, just like us, have the ability to respond with grace when they learn to depend on God. They have the ability to react with less aggression, less impulsivity, and more self-control. When we remind them that they can respond in a healthy way, they are more apt to try. It is when they embrace anxiety as an identity that we start getting into trouble.

I caution you about telling your child they "have anxiety." In this identifier, anxiety will have them. Instead, tell your child they have a mighty God who can help them fight the big feelings they feel. The goal is to empower our children with the reality that they can have soul control because God will help them. They absolutely can control the words coming out of their mouth with God's help.

- **Their Soul**

  While the other areas of control are clear, this one is a tender subject due to its invisible nature and the practice of faith. We can teach the right words to say, the right body language to use, and the thoughts that will help our children thrive. But when it comes to the soul, like we've already learned, truly it is not our job to save. We pray, share the truth, guide, lead, and encourage. But when the child lays their head on their pillow at night, they have the choice to trust God with their heart and soul or not. They are truly in charge. It is up to us to teach them so.

It goes against everything in me to tell my child they are in charge, and maybe it does for you too. After all, *I am in charge*. I say this with my chest lifted a little higher, my voice a bit stronger, and my face serious. I deeply want to control my child's world so they

> When we all surrender our souls to the Lord, letting Him have control of both the parenting and the reactions, we forge a new pathway toward peace.

don't have to hurt, struggle, or fight the battles they don't seem prepared for yet. But I am learning a different way. This script-flipping journey hasn't been easy, but living in my God-given role as the authority in my child's life and teaching them to take responsibility for their actions has served our family well. When we all surrender our souls to the Lord, letting Him have control of both the parenting and the reactions, we forge a new pathway toward peace. The key for soul control for me and my child is God's power and help in both of us.

truth-telling time

Whoever has no rule over his own spirit is like a city broken down, without walls

(PROVERBS 25:28)

The lesson we find in Proverbs 25:28 is that a person who is out of control is like a city that has been compromised. It is open to attack and has no defenses ready. The attacks are sure to come and the end is sure to be destruction.

Like the man in the psych ward who could only sling around profanity and hate, so is anyone who isn't in charge of themselves. Teaching a child they are in charge of their body, mind, words, and soul isn't teaching them to be a controlling brat over everyone around them. It teaches them that they are capable of more than what their big emotions tell them. So go ahead and tell your child the truth. Tell them they are in charge. They might look at you like you are crazy. This is the time to sit down with them and explain what it means to truly be in control of their soul. They can do it! They just might not know it yet.

☆ all-star tip

Choose an activity to do with your child such as cooking something together, doing yard work, creating something, or simply playing with play-dough or drawing. Tell your child, "You are in charge." Let them lead the time together. They get to be the teacher! Now, shift the subject and talk about soul control. Use this as a fun simple way to open the conversation to a life changing lesson.

a ray of sunshine

Dear heavenly Father, help me to realize I am in control of my emotions. I need to rely on You. Sometimes I rely on myself and react in a bad way. But I need You to help me react in a good way. Remind me that I don't always have to get my way. In Jesus' name, amen.

parent heart check

Use your journal as you consider these questions.

- Is there one area in your child's life that they have the most struggle to control? (body, mind, words, soul)
- When do you see this weakness most?

- Which area do you as a parent struggle with most? (body, mind, words, soul)

Sometimes our area and our child's area are similar. Other times they're not. But whatever your weakness, consider sharing it with your child as you both work toward growing together. Think of an activity you and your child can do together to talk about soul control. A few simple ideas are games like Red-Light Green-Light or Simon Says.

Take a moment to thank God for the strengths your child has.

game plan highlights

- Soul control is choosing to embrace the consequences of our emotional expressions.
- When a child understands and believes they are in control of their actions, reactions, body, mind, and soul, they begin to act differently.
- One of the first steps toward soul control is teaching the child, "You are in charge."
- It is teaching them that they are capable of more than what their big emotions tell them.

chapter eleven

the soul's protection of calm

"I don't want to wear glasses. Glasses are weird." When my little girl came home worried about what other people thought about her at the tender age of four, it broke this momma's heart. Bullying is nothing new and the avenues in which our children have access has increased the measures children will take to both bully and to defend themselves from such attacks. But we all know these attacks don't only come from outside the walls of our homes. Even right within the little hearts and minds of our children, they fight battles with themselves about what they look like, who they are, what they can do or can't do, especially if things don't come easily for them. For our kids who battle anxiety, these attacks are huge and regularly bombard them.

I held her toddler face close to mine and looked deeply into her bold brown eyes.

"Repeat after Mommy—I am smart."

In her sweet baby voice, she confidently said, "I am fart."

No, that was not a typo. Don't you love it when kids are learning to talk? As the mother of five with this one being my last baby, I let her say it the wrong way until she eventually corrected herself. I was sad when I finally heard her correctly get the word out like a big kid—*I am smart*. We repeated this little routine every morning.

I am smart.

I am loved.

I am wanted.

Daily, we continued to practice this little ritual. Here is the beauty. When this little child not even old enough for school would see an older sibling struggling, she knew what to do. With full confidence in herself and her knowledge of how to cope in a crisis, she approaches the sibling and says, "Take a deep breath. Smell the roses? Now, blow out the candle. Say, 'I am smart. I am loved. I am wanted.'" These words are etched into her soul because we have regularly and routinely practiced them. Now, she uses them for herself and for others.

We began this book by looking at the outside and the obvious things that affect our children. Working on external signs of anxiety is a huge accomplishment, but the goal for us as Christian parents is not to just put out the external fires for our kids. We want to enable and equip our children to fight the internal and ultimately the eternal battles on their own. The soul is the deepest part of the human. If we can reach the soul level of a child, they can learn to heal from the external and internal battles they fight.

We know Jesus can help them, but when anxiety keeps on coming, sometimes we can get weary and resort to letting things go, avoiding triggers, or making excuses due to the constant grind. We might even wrestle with our own anxiety about our child's anxiety. I see you. I hear you. I'm with you dear parent.

What do we do when we've tried literally everything, even the things in all the books, including this one?

Here is the key to calming your child's soul. Are you ready?

> If we can reach the soul level of a child, they can learn to heal from the external and internal battles they fight.

Only God can calm your child.

Only God can calm you.

Before you jump to the world's positive affirmations, attempt to get your child on track, practice coping strategies, or apply every hack in this book, there is something else. I've saved it for the end because I want you to put this book down and remember it.

Acknowledge *who* is doing the calming. It is not you and it is not me. We are the vessel God uses to guide and lead our children to calm, but we are not the calmer or the calm. **Only God can reach down into a heart and hold it steady.** We can hold a trembling body and offer security. We can wipe away tears and give assurance. We can teach coping strategies and lead a child to stop, breathe, and think. But the transformation of the body, mind, and soul only comes when God works in a child's heart. God has the power to take the wires of the brain and connect them or correct them. You and I cannot do that. So let go. Completely release the idea that this is all up to you.

It takes throwing down the weight you've carried since the day you laid eyes on that precious gift from God. When the weight of that child first pressed into your arms and on your chest, you felt it. It was heavy even when it was tiny. That is why you feel this so deeply. It's soul deep. It takes soul work to let go of that pressure. Peter gives it to us this way: "Casting all your care upon Him, for He cares for you" (1 Peter 5:7).

Soul work for you to do right now:

- Evaluate your casting skills.
- If you are still tightly gripping the idea that this is all up to you, I am giving you complete permission to let go.
- Don't just let go and do nothing.
- Let go by casting every part of this parenting struggle to God.
- Do this through prayer. Say it specifically.

Example: *Dear God, I cannot do this anymore. You know I love my child more than life, but I cannot do it by myself. I need You. I give my child and my parenting completely to You. Please show me how to do this. I give it to You. I am casting it at Your feet and I will not rely on myself. I am fully relying on You. In Jesus' name, amen.*

Once you have completely released it, you will need to regularly go back to this prayer again and again. You'll know you've picked it up again when you start telling yourself negative narratives like, *I'm messing them up* or *I'm not cut out for this.*

> If you don't have your own soul in check, you cannot impact the soul of your child effectively.

If you don't have your own soul in check, you cannot impact the soul of your child effectively. Do the work for yourself and for your child. Open God's Word. Ask Him for help. Pray. Listen. Open your heart to the voice of the only One who can offer lasting calm.

When I think of that little toddler voice proclaiming those positive words about herself and to her siblings, I think of Paul when he wrote to the church at Ephesus. In Ephesians 1, he takes almost an entire chapter to remind them who they are in Christ. Here are a few of the truths he proclaims to them about themselves:

- You are blessed
- You are chosen
- You are loved
- You are adopted
- You are accepted
- You are redeemed
- You are forgiven

While Paul begins the letter with these reminders of their identity, he closes his letter with a declaration about spiritual warfare. In Ephesians 6:10–19, he tells them to get suited up for battle and it sounds serious.

Here are the pieces of armor he instructs them to put on:

- The Full Armor of God
- The Belt of Truth
- The Breastplate of Righteousness
- The Shoes of the Gospel of Peace
- The Shield of Faith
- The Helmet of Salvation
- The Sword of the Spirit

If we were to go through each of these pieces of armor and apply them to the battle we are facing with our child's anxieties, it has the potential to change the way we do things.

The full armor of God means my child is completely covered, protected by God. The belt of truth means I will pray for my child to see truth over the lies of the enemy. The breastplate means my child's most vulnerable and important body part, the heart, is covered by God alone. The shoes mean my child with God's help can walk into hard things with peace. The shield means God is more than able to protect them better than I can. The helmet gives me comfort that God has power over the mind that is stronger than the lies and attacks of Satan. The sword, compels me to use the mighty, powerful Word of God to combat every anxiety riddled experience, lie, battle, or invisible fight and to go to war with the devil himself.

truth-telling time

Calming your anxious child is spiritual warfare that you and your child can win in God's strength. His power is what makes the difference. It might mean you teach your child to stop, breathe, and think. Or it could be simple words of repetition like "I am smart. I am loved. I am wanted." But the foundation for it all must be fought in partnership and prayer with Jesus. In John 15:5, Jesus says, "I am the vine, you are the branches. He who abides in Me, and I in him, bears much fruit; for without Me you can do nothing."

> Calming our anxious children is about carrying them to Christ over and over. Then pointing them to Him when they get too big to hold.

Aside from Christ, we will continually lose this fight for and with our children. Abide with Christ and we will win. Calming our anxious children is about carrying them to Christ over and over. Then pointing them to Him when they get too big to hold. It is realigning their sight with God's. When they are little, we work toward eyes, hands, and ears. When they get big, we pray those eyes, hands, and ears are tuned to God's voice of calm. The only way to get there is to realize the only source of calm for your anxious child is found in Christ alone for you and for your child.

☆ all-star tip

Create your own positive affirmations for you and your child. If your child is young, feel free to use our little girl's:

- I am smart.
- I am loved.
- I am wanted.

But if they are older, use Paul's from Ephesians 1:

- I am blessed.
- I am chosen.
- I am loved.
- I am adopted.
- I am accepted.
- I am redeemed.
- I am forgiven.

Feel free to create your own. If you use these or come up with your own list, reach out and share them with me. I would love to hear the calming truths you and your child are working through together.

a ray of sunshine

Dear Jesus, help me to remember that I am smart and I can make good choices. That I am loved by You. That I am wanted. That I am Your child. You Lord are the King of the whole world. When I feel like nobody likes me or like I can't do anything right, help me to rely on You. In Jesus' name, amen.

parent heart check

- The weight of parenting is heavy. Take time to write in journal your experience with parenting and the struggles you have faced.
- Letting go and still doing the work as a parent is a difficult balance. How do you think you can practice casting your child's life completely to God, but still do your part to parent?
- When we think about the armor of God, how can you practice putting this armor on yourself first before trying to defend your child?
- How can you help your child learn to defend themselves with the armor of God?
- What positive affirmations will you use with your child? When will you include this in your daily routine?

game plan highlights

- If we can reach the soul level of a child, they can learn to heal from the external and internal battles they fight.
- Only God can calm your child.
- Only God can calm you.
- Only God can reach down into a heart and hold it steady.
- If you don't have your own soul in check, you cannot impact the soul of your child effectively.

Weekly Prayer Guide for My Child's Soul

Instructions: Use the prayer guide below by praying the prayers provided or create your own.

Sunday: The Full Armor of God

God, please help my child put on the full armor of God. Protect them from the external and internal triggers that threaten to take their heart's focus off You. Give them awareness of the strength and power of Your armor. In Jesus' name, amen.

Monday: The Belt of Truth

God, please help my child put on the belt of truth. When lies of the enemy come at them with beauty and promises that are false and shallow, fill their souls with Your truth. Remind them of Your Word when wickedness is all around them. In Jesus' name, amen.

Tuesday: The Breastplate of Righteousness

God, please help my child wear the breastplate of righteousness with honor and dignity. Protect their heart from attacks that would cause them to feel swayed to bow to false idols or ideas that are contrary to Your Word. In Jesus' name, amen.

Wednesday: The Shoes of the Gospel of Peace

God, please help my child walk with the shoes of the gospel of peace. Fill their path with purpose. When the road ahead tries to steal their peace, give them boldness to walk in faith and pursue peace over the problems they see. In Jesus' name, amen.

Thursday: The Shield of Faith

God, please help my child hold firm the shield of faith. Defend them when they are attacked by other people or by their own thoughts. Shield them from the fiery darts of the enemy that try to make them believe something contrary to Your Word. In Jesus' name, amen.

Friday: The Helmet of Salvation

God, please help my child live daily in the confident helmet of Your salvation. Remind them how much You love them. Let them understand what Jesus did when He died, was buried, and rose again. Protect their minds from the doubts and fears the enemy presents. In Jesus' name, amen.

Saturday: The Sword of the Spirit

God, please help my child hold firm the sword of the Spirit. Help them commit Your Word to memory. Give them confidence in the power of Your mighty Word. Help them to respond to attacks from the enemy with the sword. Help me lead by example so they know what to do when they are surrounded. In Jesus' name, amen.

Activities for Parents & Children

Activity 8: The Soul's Source of Calm

For this activity you simply need intentional time and attention. No other supplies needed.

Instructions: Think about an activity or situation that is hard for your child.

Write it here:

____

Here are a few ideas of things that might be difficult that you could use if you can't think of something specific:

- Getting ready
- Cleaning up after themselves
- Encountering certain people
- Encountering certain animals
- Interacting with friends
- Taking a test
- Trying something new
- Going to bed

Before engaging in the activity you chose, you are going

to take a few minutes to speak directly eye to eye and hand to hand with your child. The goal is to lead your child to the realization that you are not going to help them, but God can. Be very deliberate with your words.

Example: "Tonight for bedtime, I want to give you something new to think about. If you feel like you need to get up and get Mom or you wake up and know it is not time to get up yet, say these words to yourself: *Stay and pray.*"

Say: "What should you do if you wake up and it's not time to get up yet?"

Answer: Stay and pray.

Note: We like to use hand motions for this one.

- *Stay* is one hand help up in front with palm facing the other person.
- *Pray* is hands together palm to palm.

Repeat this and practice until your child seems to understand. While this seems so simple, it is the beginning of a soul script that you can use every single night.

Say: "Mommy and Daddy might not always be with you, but God is. You can always stay and pray if you feel concerned or afraid. Let's pray right now that you will learn to stay and pray. Do you want to pray or do you want me to?"

Now pray together.

You can use a similar script like this for any activity that is difficult. You will never go wrong if you point them to God in prayer.

The next time they are getting ready to participate in a difficult activity, take the time to talk and pray with them prior to the activity.

Activity 9: The Soul's Process of Calm

Instructions: Talk about what anxiety is and how they can overcome it.

1. Ask your child direct questions.

Example: "I saw how you stood alone on the playground. How did you feel on the playground?"

2. Talk about anxiety.

Call anxiety what it is, but not in labeling the child with it as if it is something they have or someone they are. Even if there is a diagnosis, try not to use it as an excuse for the child. Use it as a tool to identify it and deal with it.

Example: "Sometimes when I am in situations that I am not sure about, I feel nervous or my heart beats really hard. Sometimes I freeze and don't know what to do, other times I just want to go home. That is called anxiety. It is something everyone deals with. But the good news is, we don't always have to feel that way and there are things that can help."

Address the answer they gave from #1.

Say: "I heard you when you said you felt [insert their answer] on the playground. I am sorry you felt that way. Let's think about some ways we can respond when we feel that way."

3. Tell them the truth.

Use the Bible as your source of truth. Do a quick google search for verses to combat the specific anxious feeling they are dealing with. For this example the feeling is lonely or left out.

Say: "The Bible says in Isaiah 41:10, 'Fear not, for I am with you; be not dismayed, for I am your God. I will strengthen you, yes, I will help you, I will uphold you with My righteous right hand.' Do you think God can help you?"

Typically a younger child will agree that God can and will help them unless they are already in a spiral out of control. Try to do this type of guiding in calmer moments or after you have helped them calm down, so they are ready to receive your words. Show them how you can take the Bible at its Word and pray with them using God's Word in your prayer.

For an older child, think of times God has helped them before. Remind them of how God has shown up for them or led them through a tough situation in the past. Thank God for it in your prayer.

Example Prayer: *God, please help [insert child's name] when they play on the playground know that You are with them. Remind them that You are holding them and that You see them even when they are alone. When I cannot help them or be right there with them, help them ask You for help because we know You help us. Thank You for always being there for me and for [insert child's name] when we are afraid or uncomfortable. In Jesus' name, amen.*

Activity 10: The Soul's Control of Calm

Instructions for the Soul's Control of Calm Activity 1: Read the poem to your child. Talk about each area they are in charge of.

Soul Control Poem

I am in charge
I have control
I can move my body
Move fast
Move slow

I am in charge
I have control
I can think good things
Happy thoughts
Be glad

I am in charge
I have control
I can say kind words
Talk right
Not bad

I am in charge
I have control
I can believe God
Trust Him
And know

Instructions for the Soul's Control of Calm Activity 2: Let the child choose an activity. If you want to, give them choices that can work well, but the ultimate decision is up to them. Narrow the activities by the categories below:

- Body
- Mind
- Words
- Soul

Activities with the body are active things like playing outside or riding a bike. You can find more ideas for these types of activities in **Part 1**.

Activities of the mind are things like gratitude practice. Let your child choose one activity from **Part 2**.

Activities for words are things like:

- Reading together or alone
- Word search puzzles
- Word games like Scrabble or Bananagrams
- The ABC game: Say a word in a specific category starting with the letter A, then B, then C and so on.
- Practice typing on the computer
- Texting a friend or family member
- Writing a list, story, or note

Note: The goal here is to focus on words in some way and let your child be confident that they can choose an activity and succeed at it. If your child is not a great reader and they get frustrated with reading, encourage them toward something else for this activity. Or simply read aloud one of their favorite books to them.

Activities for the soul:

- Journaling or talking about what happened today
- Journaling or talking about what went well and what was difficult
- Drawing a picture of a favorite Bible character
- Drawing comics of Bible stories
- Reading the Bible
- Reading a devotion
- Listening to the Bible or a biblical podcast or audiobook
- Making a prayer list
- Writing a prayer
- Praying out loud
- Journaling prayers

soul check

Use this template to guide your child through a soul check each day:

What made you feel happy today?

What made you feel sad?

What made you feel anxious?

What did you do when you felt like that?

If you could change something about today, what would it be?

Name or draw one person you are thankful for today.

Name or draw one thing you are thankful for today.

Activity 11: The Soul's Protection of Calm

Instructions for the Soul's Protection of Calm Activity 1: Have your child do as much of this activity on their own as possible. This is a good opportunity for you to step back and empower them to take ownership.

- Take a photo of your child.
- Print it out.
- Use the icons below to trace each piece of armor on white paper.
- Color or paint armor.
- Cut out and glue each piece of armor on the child's photo.
- With each piece of armor applied, talk about how each piece protects us and helps us defend against anxious ideas and fears.

The Full Armor of God

- The Belt of Truth
- The Breastplate of Righteousness
- The Shoes of the Gospel of Peace
- The Shield of Faith
- The Helmet of Salvation
- The Sword of the Spirit

Instruction for the Soul's Protection of Calm Activity 2:
Read the poem to your child and talk about the armor of God and how it prepares and protects them for the daily spiritual battles we all face.

The Full Armor of God Poem

I want to suit up for war
Put on the belt of truth
I want to soar

Guarded by the breastplate
Righteousness all over my heart
I want to get off to a good start

Walking in peace
Wearing Jesus shoes
I want to be ready to wisely choose

With a shield all around me
Blocking attacks
I am choosing to not look back

My mind is steady
With salvation and joy
For each attack I am ready

My weapon is stable
The Sword of the Spirit
With God's Truth I know I am able

For printed versions of all activities, go to MicahMaddox.com

acknowledgments

This book has been on my heart for a while, but living in the middle of it seemed like a good reason to put it on the shelf and revisit it long into the future. But God had other plans. When the opportunity came up to share my thoughts on this topic, I wrestled day and night if this was the right time.

God woke me in the middle of the night and gave me the clear answer. Within days we had a plan and the book came to life faster than I ever dreamed. It could have never happened without my Savior's calm and direct guidance, tender voice, and clear instruction. Thank You, Lord, for helping me sift through my muddy thoughts and intense feelings on this subject matter.

Thank you, Rob, for letting me read aloud portions over and over to see if it needed tweaking or more insight, thought, or polish. You've not only listened, you've lived this with me, and I can't thank you enough for being a huge source of calm to my chaos. Thank you to my children, for letting me share our stories and our lives with others in hopes of offering hope. Thank you for letting me try and fail and try again applying the things God continues to teach me.

Thank you to my literary agent, Tracie Miles, for believing in me and helping me find my next steps and this book.

Thank you to Erin, Avrie, and the amazing team at Moody Publishers for championing this message and cheering me on along the way.

Thank you, Mom, for being my beta reader and for praying for this message and walking through this journey with me. Thank you to my friends and literary experts Sarah Frazer and Tara Dotson for reading first drafts and helping me find the places that needed attention or direction.

And lastly, thank you, Ray, for teaching me that behavior isn't always a sign of rebellion but a signal that something needs attention and redirection. With you, I've learned to see anxiety as an assignment to slow down and understand. Stop, breathe, and think. Thumbs up, buddy. God is taking good care of us.

notes

Chapter 1: Seeking Calm

1. David Thomas, *Raising Emotionally Strong Boys: Tools Your Son Can Build On for Life* (Baker Publishing Group, 2022), 66.

2. Tamara L. Goldsby, PhD, "The Amazing Power of 3 Deep Breaths," *Psychology Today*, updated May 20, 2025, https://www.psychologytoday.com/us/blog/less-stress-more-peace/202505/the-amazing-power-of-3-deep-breaths.

3. Howard E. LeWine, "Understanding the Stress Response," Harvard Health, April 3, 2024, https://www.health.harvard.edu/staying-healthy/understanding-the-stress-response.

4. Andrew Weil, "Breathing: An Introduction," https://www.drweil.com/health-wellness/body-mind-spirit/stress-anxiety/breathing-an-introduction/.

Chapter 2: Magnetic Words

1. Karyn B. Purvis, David R. Cross, and Wendy Lyons Sunshine, *The Connected Child: Bring Hope and Healing to Your Adoptive Family* (McGraw Hill, 2007), 25.

2. Josh McDowell, "Rules Without Relationships Lead to Rebellion," Sightline, https://sightlineministry.org/assets/rules-without-relationships-lead-to-rebellion/.

Chapter 3: Building Connection

1. Jenna Fletcher, "The Psychology Behind Prolonged Eye Contact and Intimacy," Psychcentral.com, July 12, 2024, https://psychcentral.com/relationships/prolonged-eye-contact#benefits.

2. Ibid.

3. Roland Rotz, PhD, "How Does Fidgeting Enhance Focus for Individuals with ADHD?," CHADD.org February 2025, https://chadd.org/attention-article/how-does-fidgeting-enhance-focus-for-individuals-with-adhd/.

4. Karyn B. Purvis, David R. Cross, and Wendy Lyons Sunshine, *The Connected Child: Bring Hope and Healing to Your Adoptive Family* (McGraw Hill, 2007), 78.

5. Ibid, 183.

6. Becky A. Bailey, PhD, *I Love You Rituals* (HarperCollins, 2000), 8.

Chapter 4: Moving Memories

1. "Fight, Flight, or Freeze," Harvard Health, https://www.health.harvard.edu/mindscape/for-young-people/brain-body-connection/fight-flight-or-freeze.

2. David Thomas, *Raising Emotionally Strong Boys: Tools Your Son Can Build On for Life* (Baker Publishing Group, 2022), 21.

3. "Exercise for Stress and Anxiety," Anxiety & Depression Association of America, https://adaa.org/living-with-anxiety/managing-anxiety/exercise-stress-and-anxiety.

4. Jonathan Haidt, *The Anxious Generation: How the Great Rewiring of Childhood Is Causing an Epidemic of Mental Illness* (Penguin Press, 2024), 27.

5. John J. Ratey, MD, "Can Exercise Help Treat Anxiety?," Harvard Health, October 24, 2019, https://www.health.harvard.edu/blog/can-exercise-help-treat-anxiety-2019102418096.

6. David Mathis, "In Him We Live and Move: Stewarding a Body in Sedentary Times," *Desiring God*, September 20, 2020, https://www.desiringgod.org/articles/in-him-we-live-and-move#2-to-jumpstart-joy.

7. "How to Reduce Stress and Anxiety Through Movement and Mindfulness," Harvard Health, August 11, 2025, https://www.health.harvard.edu/mind-and-mood/how-to-reduce-stress-and-anxiety-through-movement-and-mindfulness.

Chapter 5: Learning What-Is Statements

1. Jennie Allen, *Get Out of Your Head: Stopping the Spiral of Toxic Thoughts* (WaterBrook, 2020), 10.
2. Jenna Fletcher, "6 Ways to Stop a Worry-Filled What-If Cycle," PsychCentral, updated March 17, 2022, https://psychcentral.com/anxiety/ways-to-stop-a-worry-filled-what-if-cycle#therapy.
3. Max Lucado, *Anxious for Nothing: Finding Calm in a Chaotic World* (HarperCollins, 2017), 4.

Chapter 6: Practicing Gratitude

1. Ron Rapee et al., *Helping Your Anxious Child, Third Edition: A Step-by-Step Guide for Parents* (New Harbinger Publications, Inc., 2022), 29.
2. Joshua Brown and Joel Wong, "How Gratitude Changes You and Your Brain," *Greater Good Magazine*, June 6, 2017, https://greatergood.berkeley.edu/article/item/how_gratitude_changes_you_and_your_brain.

Chapter 7: Transforming Thoughts

1. Catherine M. Pittman, PhD, Elizabeth M. Karle, MLIS, *Rewire Your Anxious Brain: How to Use the Neuroscience of Fear to End Anxiety, Panic, and Worry* (New Harbinger Publications, 2015), 285.
2. Max Lucado, *Anxious for Nothing: Finding Calm in a Chaotic World* (HarperCollins, 2017), 103.

Chapter 9: The Soul's Process of Calm

1. "Sleep Terrors," Mayo Clinic, https://www.mayoclinic.org/diseases-conditions/sleep-terrors/symptoms-causes/syc-20353524.
2. Julie Radico, "Avoidance Maintains Anxiety," *Psychology Today*, September 7, 2024, https://www.psychologytoday.com/us/blog/you-are-enough/202409/avoidance-maintains-anxiety.
3. Charles F. Stanley, *Handle with Prayer: Unwrap the Source of God's Strength for Living* (David C. Cook, 2015), 60.

4. Alice Robb, “People Say It’s Boring to Talk About a Dream You Had. Here’s Why You Should Do It Anyway,” *TIME*, November 16, 2018, https://time.com/5456903/why-we-dream-alice-robb/.

Chapter 10: The Soul’s Control of Calm

1. Maureen Salamon, “Co-Regulation: Helping Children and Teens Navigate Big Emotions,” Harvard Health, April 3, 2024, https://www.health.harvard.edu/blog/co-regulation-helping-children-and-teens-navigate-big-emotions-202404033030.

a parent's blessing

By Micah Maddox

You've given me this child
A gift from God above
You've created every detail
With uniqueness and with love

You knew from the beginning
Every season we would face
You know today the challenges
The struggles of this race

With all the things we hold
And with every single test
We ask for your presence
To give us peace and rest

Calm assurance of your grace
Sure blessing day by day
A stillness of the soul
And mercy for today

let's stay connected!

Connect with Micah on Instagram for encouragement and updates on everyday life.

@mrsmicah

more by

micah maddox

Instructional videos

Prayer calendars

Activities for you and your child

And more!

Find it at MicahMaddox.com.